Courageous Women of the Prairie

of the Prairie

Volume 1

Courageous Women of Hope in God

DEDICATION

This book is dedicated to the reader, especially the children, women and men who are survivors of child sexual abuse.

May you know God intimately and become the person He created you to be through, with and in Jesus Christ, the Shepherd of our souls.

And after you have suffered a little while, the God of all grace, who has called you to his eternal glory in Christ, will himself restore, confirm, strengthen, and establish you.
~1 Peter 5:10~

CONTENTS

ACKNOWLEDGMENTS

A SPECIAL THANK YOU TO those who had the courage to tell their story and to those who provided prayers and support, which were essential in taking this project from conception to reality. I am especially appreciative of:

Coleen Ehresmann, Hope In God Publisher's Assistant, Watertown, South Dakota, for your openness to this project.

Joy Nelson, Founder of Joy Ranch and Owner of Haugan and Nelson Realty, Watertown, South Dakota, for your unwavering faith in and continuous support of this project.

Sherray Hurlbert, Hope In God Contemplative Writing Instructor and Instructor of Lake Area Technical Institute, Watertown, South Dakota, for exposing yourself to heart wrenching stories of child sexual abuse, for teaching survivors how to write their stories and for coaching them through the writing process until completion.

Barbara Younger, Hope In God Contemplative Art Instructor and Sister of Mother of God Monastery, Watertown, South Dakota, for teaching survivors how to express themselves through watercolors and for allowing the Holy Spirit to guide and direct your pencil and brush for each survivor's story and the cover of this book.

Janine Rew-Werling, Hope In God Fireside Chat Pastor and Pastor of Hosanna Lutheran Church, Watertown, South Dakota, for sharing God's Word, your life experiences with survivors of child sexual abuse, and for allowing the Holy Spirit to guide and direct you to annotate Scripture for each survivor's story contained within this book.

Jan DeBerg, Shelly Ebbers, Angie Meseberg, Joy Nelson, Sara Nelson, Julie Stevenson, Diane Stiles, Tim Toomey and Barbara Younger, Hope In God Advisory Board, for your guidance, direction and ongoing support.

Carol Ford, Judith Fischer, Donna Gast, Cindy Geier, Hawa Kamara, and Mavis Kemnitz, Hope In God Prayer Warriors for your continuous prayers and support.

Nancy Adair, Christine Berger, Susan Buhler, LisaLyn Castonguay, Kara Julius, Jessica McClanahan and Miranda Redday, Hope In God Spiritual Leadership Team, for your willingness to serve and give of yourselves to others in the name of Jesus Christ.

Steve Biswell, Paul Kimball, Shawn McCall, and Hans Sacrison, Hope In God for Men, for your prayers and support of the children, women and the many men who have been harmed and wounded by child sexual abuse.

Janet Brage, Jennifer Brudwick, and Scottie Hagen, Hope In God Circle Leaders, for continuing to grow our ministry throughout northeast South Dakota as we wrote this book.

Denis Meier and Emily Meisel, spiritual advisors, for ongoing support and prayers.

Tony Vitek, my husband, for supporting me and giving me your time to complete this book.

Jesus Christ, for saving me.

Jo Vitek
Colossians 1:27

HOW THIS CAME TO BE

God called me into ministry when I was 15 years old, but I had to wait until I was 55 years old for God to resurrect my calling for His glory. I had no idea God would bring my dream back to life. In my ignorance, I put a "period" where God wanted me to place a "comma." When I joined the Columbus Police Department in 1977, I forsook God's call to be a minister. Although I gave up on God, He never gave up on me. At the time of my calling, I wasn't ready for the dream God had given me. I needed to spend 36 years in law enforcement—as "time in the desert" for God to bend and prune me. It was there God opened my eyes and ears and gave me experiences to transform my heart fashioning me to be able to fulfill my dream—His purpose.

In 2005, God led my husband, Tony and I to Watertown, South Dakota where I assumed the position of Chief of Police for 8 years. During my law enforcement career, I've made plenty of connections and planned to teach and consult upon retiring. But my plans didn't align with God's purpose. But the truth of the matter is, unless God ordains a plan, it can't be done. Now, I know God had to take me into the past before I could accomplish His purpose. I needed to go back and experience God's grace before I could go forward.

Over the past four years, God has been revealing a dream to me. It's His purpose for my life and for yours. My legacy won't be about me but how God used me to help you—those who are wounded and broken because of child sexual abuse. God has been spoon-feeding His plan to me, piece by piece. First, God called me back into the pulpit through Pastor Janine Rew-Werling of the Hosanna Lutheran Church in the Winter of 2013. I love passage from the Book of Ephesians (3:7-13):

> *Of this gospel I have become a servant according to the gift of God's grace that was given me by the working of his power. ⁸ Although I am the very*

least of all the saints, this grace was given to me to bring to the Gentiles the news of the boundless riches of Christ, ⁹ and to make everyone see what is the plan of the mystery hidden for ages in God who created all things; ¹⁰ so that through the church the wisdom of God in its rich variety might now be made known to the rulers and authorities in the heavenly places. ¹¹ This was in accordance with the eternal purpose that he has carried out in Christ Jesus our Lord, ¹² in whom we have access to God in boldness and confidence through faith in him. ¹³ I pray therefore that you may not lose heart over my sufferings for you; they are your glory.

Robert Louis Stevenson said, "To be what we are, and to become all that we can become, is the only end of life." This is the end and the ultimate purpose of my life and yours, to make known to all the unsearchable riches of Jesus Christ. So, our objective is to be a faithful servant of His. The Apostle Paul said, "Of this gospel I have become a servant." but what does it mean to be a servant? What goes into our making? It has to start with "the gift of God's grace." We are recipients of God's grace through Jesus Christ. And isn't that the starting place for all of us—whether we be clergy or lay? Whether we are Assembly of God, Church of Christ, Baptist, Catholic, Christian Alliance, Congregationalist, E-Free, Lutheran, Methodist, Wesleyan, or otherwise. Just as the apostle said, "There is 'One Lord, One Faith, One Baptism, One God and Father of all who is over all and through all and in all'" (Ephesians 4:5-6).

God called Tony and I to create Chief Jo's Hope, Healing and Hoof Prints in Winter of 2016 and Hope In God for Women in the Summer of 2016. Hope In God is a Christian network of women survivors of child sexual abuse and sexual assault who provide spiritual and emotional support to each other while increasing community awareness in Northeast South Dakota. God never works just through one individual. He always works through a community of individuals to accomplish His purpose.

Hope In God serves as a resource for law enforcement and churches and provides six offerings to survivors of child sexual abuse and sexual assault: weekly Wounded Heart book study; one-on-one mentoring offering; outreach awareness opportunities for churches, businesses, schools and organizations; indoor and outdoor activities; weekly circle groups; and, diversity initiatives.

In February 2017, the first-ever Hope In God Winter Retreat occurred at Joy Ranch. The women who attended were 18 to 83 years old. Various spiritually-based offerings were provided and included a *Contemplative Writing* experience, in which survivors learned how to write their stories with anonymity. Sherray Hulbert of Lake Area Technical Institute of Watertown, South Dakota instructed the course. Sherray uncovered the secrets to great story writing for the women. She taught them the tricks that all good story writers use when they tell their story. Then, she gave them the time to begin planning and writing their own story, which allowed them to practice their newly discovered writing techniques. The women left the retreat and began working on their stories.

We share a common destiny—God's ultimate purpose is to bring us into full relationship with Him while forming us into the image of His son, Jesus Christ. We also have a unique destiny because we're each "one of a kind." There will never be another you. God gifted you with uniqueness and He wants you to become the very best version of you. You'll discover the best version you as you journey seeking God with all your heart, mind, soul and strength.

Fourteen women took that journey. Courageously, they went into their past. They faced and conquered their fears so they could move forward with their lives to become the very best version of themselves. Their stories are real. This is the first-ever publication of Courageous Women of the Prairie. The book will help us to raise funds for future Hope In God retreats at Joy Ranch.

You might say that God created Hope In God to be a dreamcatcher—come share your hope and dreams with us and we'll help you to become the very best you that God created. My dream is not about me but how God will use us through Hope In God to help others, especially, those who have been wounded by child sexual abuse. Courageous Women of the Prairie is God writing His story through, with, and in us.

Jo Vitek
June 25, 2017

Romans 5:2-5

Psalm 143

My Soul Thirsts for You

Hear my prayer, O Lord;
   give ear to my pleas for mercy!
   In your faithfulness answer me, in your righteousness!
Enter not into judgment with your servant,
   for no one living is righteous before you.
For the enemy has pursued my soul;
   he has crushed my life to the ground;
   he has made me sit in darkness like those long dead.
Therefore my spirit faints within me;
   my heart within me is appalled.
I remember the days of old;
   I meditate on all that you have done;
   I ponder the work of your hands.
I stretch out my hands to you;
   my soul thirsts for you like a parched land.
Answer me quickly, O Lord!
   My spirit fails!
Hide not your face from me,
   lest I be like those who go down to the pit.
Let me hear in the morning of your steadfast love,
   for in you I trust.
Make me know the way I should go,
   for to you I lift up my soul.
Deliver me from my enemies, O Lord!
   I have fled to you for refuge.
Teach me to do your will,
   for you are my God!
Let your good Spirit lead me
   on level ground!
For your name's sake, O Lord, preserve my life!
   In your righteousness bring my soul out of trouble!
And in your steadfast love you will cut off my enemies,
   and you will destroy all the adversaries of my soul,
   for I am your servant.

"It is going to take a lot of work
walking on this journey being
a survivor Instead of a victim,
but it is well worth every step."

"He drew me up from the pit of destruction, out of the miry bog, and set my feet upon a rock, making my steps secure."

Psalm 40:2

Carol's Story

When does one's story really begin? At birth? Or perhaps our first memory? I don't recall having a lot of happy memories or even plain memories from my childhood. I now wonder if the memory lapses are a self-defense mechanism, so I won't think about the bad. The last few weeks of writing my story have brought forth many reasons why I think I had purposefully forgotten so much. There is only so much unhappy a person wants to think about, so you just push and push and push it down to some deep dark place.

I had been trying and retrying to write this and just couldn't seem to get the words to flow, and then finally it hit me. Duh! I wasn't giving this over to God and praying before starting.

Growing up, I can't remember our house being anything but a violent house. Punishment for anything and everything was swift and mean. What I mean by *mean* was that it wasn't scolding or grounding or having things taken away, it was, instead, a good spanking that evolved into a good beating for even the smallest of misdeeds. If the one who did the wrong did not confess (and honestly who would?), we got lined up and all got it. Being the youngest, I was usually last in the lineup, and by the time mom got around to me, her arm would start to get so tired that she had to catch me. Our house had all rooms connected by at least one if not two doors, and if it was your lucky day, none of them were closed to slow you down.

First came the screaming and then came the screaming and the beating. You just knew if she was yelling what would be coming next. Once it was for some stupid thing dad did and didn't make right before he left for work. Of course we all denied knocking her precious decorative towel off the top of the fridge. For once it wasn't one of us. Well, we all got our due beating. Dad came home and said he had done it and was going to move the fridge out and get it when he got home. I remember her saying,

"Well, you probably all deserved the spanking for something else anyways." Our spankings progressed from the hand to wood laths and then to a belt with the buckle cut off. And it wasn't just a few smacks, it was just like she couldn't stop. The sound of the pantry door opening and the belt being whipped off the pencil sharpener brought such fear my stomach would hurt. To this day the sound of a belt being pulled too quickly through belt loops on pants can still send a shiver up my spine. It was a way of life.

I wasn't fully dressed unless I was sporting bruises on my arms and legs. Once she got me across the mouth with the belt, and my bottom lip was huge-no hiding that, so I told those who asked that I slipped and fell. Classic excuse. Fear and violence. Violence and fear. Around and around it went every day after day after day. Was it any wonder I wet the bed until age eight and sucked my thumb?

I lived always trying so hard to please, and if that didn't work, I tried as hard as possible to just be invisible. I never felt safe or loved. Quite early on, the parental physical and mental abuse carried over into sibling physical abuse. It was to be expected, I guess, considering that was how we lived every day of our lives. I was the youngest, so you can about guess where I stood in the pecking order. That and being a scrawny little thing, I didn't stand a chance against my older brother and sister. Tattling did absolutely no good. Mom in all her wisdom would just say we needed to learn how to get along. Oh how I came to hate that phrase- even more so when I became an adult. Tattling turned out to be a bad idea anyway since the retaliation was much worse than the original offense, so it just became easier and less painful to just give in and suck it up. This has continued into my adult life, easily being the victim especially to my siblings who at times could make life a living hell and Mom telling me I need to learn to get along.

School really was no different. The fear of being wrong kept me from ever raising my hand. Fear of being laughed at kept me from trying to make friends and trying to explain away the bruises all over my body. What if they figured out what went on in our house? The idea of anyone knowing was so shameful I didn't want anyone to notice me or befriend me.

A particularly disturbing memory came to me not that long ago as I was trying for the umpteenth time to write this story. It is hard to think about a parent being so horrifically cruel. I was pretty young, and we had all been outside for a long period of time building a snow fort. When we finally came in for the day, we went straight to the basement to take off our boots, coats and snow pants, so we wouldn't make a mess in the back entry and steps.

Mom came downstairs and went completely ballistic because our inner clothes were wet also. She started scolding which quite quickly escalated to yelling, never stopping as we took off our pants and hung them on the clothes line. The screaming continued to escalate as she grabbed some sort of board off the table saw and starting beating the living crap out of us. You can only imagine the pain that board caused striking bare skin that was already so red from being so cold. The pain was so excruciating, I couldn't even walk. I crawled up the basement stairs on my hands and knees and crawled under my bed and sobbed. I begged to God to please, please, please let my real parents come and find me and save me, or at least make this mean mom die. This would not be the last time such a horrific beating would occur.

I am reminded daily of an incident where she was beating me then threw me against the edge of a drawer that was at the bottom of the closet. My back looked like a mottled grape jelly sandwich for days and days, and the pain was unthinkable. Of course after the bruising went away, they sent me to a chiropractor constantly and nothing was ever mentioned about how this back pain happened. Ten or so years ago I had an MRI, and it was discovered I have bulging discs in the L3, L4, and L5 region, an old hairline fracture, and a fracture of the vertebrae which is the reason for my continuous back pain. I guess it is the gift that keeps on giving from her. I wonder if she even remembers the things she did to us or even ever thinks back on it. How could she not? My siblings suffered some even worse beatings at the hands of my father. It is a wonder to me that one of us didn't die from some of the beatings that were handed out.

It is easy to see why sibling abuse started. It was learned young in life that violence was an accepted thing. Dad preached to us constantly that bad things that happen to a person were their due punishment from God. We were brought up with fire and brimstone and never missed church for any reason. It was very important that everyone saw we were in church every Sunday, and on the way home it was a constant commentary from Dad about who wasn't there. Being seen in church was what was important to him. I don't think it was the message. We were never taught about a loving God.

One of the first things I did when I left home was to just quit going to church. I never received a message of hope, love, or forgiveness but one of hopelessness, and I was going to burn in hell. As a child I didn't think my life could get any worse than it was, but it did.

My brother first molested me at about age 10. Many times followed the first, but none of those instances are as clear as the first. Mom was outside hanging laundry. I could see her outside the bedroom window. He had me pinned down on his bed with his hand over my mouth. I couldn't breathe. "Oh please. I can't breathe. Let me up. What are you doing? Mom! Mom!" My mind kept screaming, "Help me. Oh please. Someone, please help me. Help me." Of course no one could hear. His hand was over my mouth. I was just screaming in my mind. Afterwards, he squeezed his hands around my throat and kept squeezing, and I fought as hard as I could to get his hands off but couldn't. He then promised me if I ever told, he would get me by the throat and not let go until I was dead. There were so many times over the last 48 years I wish he had squeezed until I was dead. What he did to me at that time in the space of just a few minutes defined who I was to become.

To this day I don't like to be in any circumstance where I feel like I may not be able to breathe. Stupid.I know. Driving across a bridge. If I had an accident and went in the water, then I wouldn't be able to breathe. What an irrational fear! Or a closed-in room like an elevator or any closed-in or tight space. It all makes me feel like I can't breathe. And I think it all stems back to that day when I couldn't breathe. That was his favorite thing to do to me as he molested me every time- cover my mouth and nose and choke me as he threatened to kill me if I told. He had an evilness in him, and every day I feared but also hated him more. I had a lot of anger and hate towards my mom too. How could she not know what in the heck was going on in her own house? I can look at this now and know she didn't have a clue. She was so naïve in the ways of life.

I began a true hatred for life and a love affair with food at this point in my life. Over my teenage years I would hide away in my room for hours on end with books and candy bars or chips, whatever my babysitting money could afford. If I needed to get away, I would live at the library for hours on end. Anything to get away from my brother, sister and home. By this time my brother was so in trouble with everything that much of my parents' attention was on him and his misdoings, and I was lucky enough to just go unnoticed. As time went by, it became easier to stay out of my brother's path, and one day he died. I thought, "Yay! It is over, and my life will be good from now on." That was a naïve thought from a naïve teenager. What he did to me has defined the rest of my life. I had such self-contempt and hatred for me and my family. As far as I could see, nothing good had ever come from being around them. I stayed away as much as possible, but then guilt would take over, and I would spend time with them just to come away feeling like "the nobody" I was so sure I was.

In my younger years, time with my grandma was my only salvation. After Grandpa passed, every summer I got to stay with her, and it was like heaven. She was the most loving and caring person. It was like she knew what went on at home, and this was her way of trying to make it better. She didn't possess a mean bone in her body, nor did she have a bad thing to say about anyone or anything. Her kindness and love were the only things that kept me going. I miss her all the time. I asked her one day why Dad was so mean-talking to her all the time, and she just answered, "You never talk back to him." I didn't like the way he talked to her but was too scared to say anything to him. That was the way he always was with Mom too. It was confusing to a young girl, but I vowed if I ever got married, it wasn't going to be to someone who was like him. I always dreaded when school was starting again. That meant I was headed back home never knowing what was going to happen day to day.

I was quite young when I developed ulcers and was on medication. One of the meds was valium. In those days they didn't have refill restrictions. You could just take it in whenever, and it was filled with no questions asked. On three different occasions I remember feeling so desolate and incapable of dealing anymore that I just took all of the pills in the bottle, and then I would get scared and make myself throw them all up. What a chicken! I couldn't even do that right. I thought about death all the time and how it must be better than living the life I was living. How does one deal and go on with life? The best you can. But . . . it didn't work.

I have spent years fighting with my addiction to food as my comfort using it in any and all situations, trying every diet known to man, taking drastic measures to lose but never dealing with the true issues that led to the eating and destructive behavior.

I was lucky enough to find an amazing man who became my husband and best friend-everything a woman could ever want, and I still couldn't deal with my demons. We were together for almost fifteen years before I had the courage to share with him about my brother molesting me, but I still didn't deal with it in the way that I should have. He learned bits and pieces of my life and childhood as the years went on, but I never got down into the nitty gritty of specifics of the abuse we endured as children or things that my brother did to me.

As our marriage went on, I continued to have problems with my siblings. I would take their verbal abuse so long and tell them off or shut them out. Then the phone call from Mom would come telling me I needed to learn how to get along with my sisters. With my self-esteem so low for all of my life, I was an easy target for just about anyone who liked to be a bully. Staying away from family as much as possible or just giving in was the easy and cowardly way out, but I think with everything that happened to me as a child, I was full of self-contempt, anger, hate, worthlessness and despair.

Then one day while on Facebook I read a story, and my life changed. I thought, "Wow! How brave of this amazing woman to share her story with others on Facebook of all places." I shared back with her. She invited me to a retreat out to the hill with Sister Emily, and my life began to change. I will be forever grateful for this amazing woman coming into my life and showing me that by God's grace, my life could and would change for the good. "It's all good" is one of her favorite sayings I think. I had been living but not really living for many years, going to church but not really being present or accepting of God. I was not asking God to come into me and my life and lead me the way that He wanted me to go. I had been struggling with the God thing for so long, and I now know that is the first step in healing on this journey of mine.

I would be lying if I said this hasn't been hard trying to get this written. I have fallen back into some of the old habits and struggled my way out. Binge eating. Staying away from people. Hiding at home. A lot of tears have been shed over the last couple of days thinking back to the way things were. I could recount so many things that happened that made me what I am today. I have been a victim of one kind or another for so many years, and sometimes it just makes me tired, and I want it all to go away, but it won't. I have felt so alone for so long. Thank you, God, for Jo and HIG who have made it possible for so many to see we are not walking this path alone. I have become more accepting of the fact that my relationships with family members will never be like that of some families, but that is okay. You can't pick your family, but you don't need to let them think it is okay to treat you as they want. It is ok to refuse to be treated in a way that is unacceptable. I have been a victim for many years but am now a survivor, a warrior, a Hope in God Warrior.

I found this prayer in a book a few days ago and it kind of says it all for me.

I have been floundering with my faith for
so long, floundering with my life, not knowing how

to take it in a good direction, feeling lost, sometimes hopelessly lost.

Jesus, I invite you into my life and everything that I am. I'm not even fully sure what this means, but I ask you to make me alive again. Jesus, I come and I'm broken. I'm restless. I'm empty. My heart is angry and bitter. I'm hurting. I'm grieving, Lord. Today it feels like a part of me, like all of me is dead. God, if it's possible, just as you did with Jesus, would you please bring me back to life? I don't want to be this person anymore. Lord, if it's possible from the inside out, would you please make me new? Please forgive me. Please take control of my life. Starting today, I long to follow and have a relationship with you.

Know that God loves you, no matter what and is patiently always waiting for you to ask Him into your heart. What can be more amazing than that broken, tattered you? He loves you for you.

It's going to take time and a lot of work walking on this journey being a survivor instead of a victim, but it is well worth every step.

Praise be to God.
P.S. Thanks, Jo.

"Anyone who continually struggles with something, whether it be depression, addiction or any obstacle, over and over again probably needs to ask God to reveal the root of the problem and then take it to His courts."

"...for he has said, I will never leave you nor forsake you. So we can confidently say, The Lord is my helper; I will not fear; what can man do to me?"
Job 19:25-28

Lisel's Story

"What is this? What's happening? Why am I sitting on the edge of the bed, leaning over with my hands on the old vanity dresser with my heart racing, and my breathing so hard? And why do I feel like I'm going to throw up?" My foggy mind questioned as I awoke in this confused state...there was no crisis...my husband slept peacefully...the house was quiet. There were no memories of a nightmare even though my body was reacting as such.

A few weeks later the same thing happened, but this time I was running down the hallway, flicked on the living room light and collapsed into the swivel chair...heart pounding, breathing hard and feeling sick to my stomach.

One morning when I awoke feeling sick and just plain "icky" throughout my entire being (a feeling that would last throughout the day), I realized I've had this feeling before. In fact, throughout my entire adult life, every once in a while, I had this same dream in which I'd wake up feeling sick like this...a sickness that hung around the entire day.

Throughout my life, debilitating depression and anxiety oppressed me, so I sought help. Counselors and doctors told me I had all the symptoms of sexual abuse, but I had no memories of such a thing. I just knew my entire life has been a struggle filled with extreme anxiety, panic attacks and depression affecting every area of my functioning in this world. I wasn't like everyone else...I couldn't hold a job without extreme anxiety; being around people was overwhelming and exhausting.

Even though I had accepted Jesus Christ as my savior at the age of 16, the fear and anxiety would not leave. I didn't dare share my struggles with my new-found Christian family because after all, something was wrong with me, and I had to pretend I was "normal." My mother also taught me people didn't really care ... they were just being polite. With no one in my life who would allow me to be real and share my distress during my entire life, I had to suppress and deny everything since I was born. The anguish grew and established itself firmly, and the poison spread more and more throughout my being. Every day was a struggle for survival...day after day after day after year after year after year after....

Besides sexual abuse, I came to realize that I had grown up in a home saturated with polluted sex, hatred, alcoholism, mental illness, manipulation, gaslighting, self-absorption, narcissism, mind games, paranoia, neglect, brain washing, lying, mixed messages, control, emotional abuse...even to the point of not being able to get anyone's attention when my physical body was dying at nine years old...I was terrified, but it was not the first or only time I was terrified. I started experiencing full-blown panic attacks from the age of eight years old (although I didn't know there was a name for them and thought I was surely dying).

Consequently, my entire life was crippled by anxiety and distrust. Jobs overwhelmed me...panic attacks were commonplace...they always escalated until I would black out (but not fall down) and then slowly come back down. By this time, I had learned to cover them up (because I knew this was not normal), so well that the people I worked with who stood right in front of me during a panic attack, did not even know I was having one. I pushed myself to have a job until the anxiety caused my head to separate from my body and float about a foot above me. So, then I bore the shame of not being employed (the first question everyone asks is, "Where do you work?")

After years of counseling, self-help and learning about myself, I finally realized the only true healing and peace I'll ever find is in Jesus Christ. Even though I'd been a born-again Christian for many years, I tried to live a "religious" life instead...I didn't understand exactly what Jesus had done for me. It was like I had been saved, but now I had to keep from losing that salvation. I thought I had to make myself Christ-like instead of releasing the Christ life from within. I had no idea the entire reason Jesus died was because I could NOT be perfect and righteous on my own. I'm still trying to let that sink in and actually believe that...in my heart, not just my head.

I misinterpreted what "sin" was...it's not a list of rules to follow...it's being in bondage because of separation from the God who created me and loves me more than any human on earth could. Because I didn't understand, I once again stuffed everything inside pretending I was normal and "righteous." Besides, my mom had taught me that people don't really care and don't really want to know how you're doing and that I must hide everything that makes me look imperfect-always pretend everything is OK.

A few years ago, I quit watching TV (which used to be my only refuge) because the shows...the commercials...everything became so disgusting and upsetting to me. Now, I am filling my mind with the things of God. Every day I listen online to messages of how much God loves me and what God's Grace is all about. As it says in Romans 10:17 (New Living Translation): "So faith comes from hearing, that is hearing the Good News about Christ." I really believe what I allow into my mind forms/shapes me, so I am very careful what I allow inside.

Years ago, I was baptized in the Holy Spirit with the evidence of speaking in tongues as is recorded in Acts 2:4, "And they were all filled with the Holy Spirit and began to speak in other tongues as the Spirit gave them utterance." I heard someone say she prays in tongues more than she does in English...I hadn't thought of that before. I began to yield to the Holy Spirit by bypassing the brain and letting my spirit pray as often as I was nudged. I have learned what a tremendous gift this is...it even relieves anxiety...the Spirit knows what to pray as it says in Romans 8:26, "The Spirit also joins to help in our weakness because we do not know what to pray for as we should, but the Spirit Himself intercedes for us with unspoken groanings." I love to walk in the country praying in the Spirit...it's as if we are walking amongst His creation together. "For the promise [of the Holy Spirit] is to *and* for you and your children, and to *and* for all that are far away, [even] to *and* for as many as the Lord our God invites *and* bids to come to Himself."

Things are far from perfect in my life, but I have a supernatural peace....the peace that passes all understanding...as long as I keep my focus on Jesus. When I start to look at the circumstances or fill my head with other things, the depression and anxiety return. My healing is in Jesus. John 10:10, "Jesus came so that I may have life and have it to the full!" I feel like I may finally be catching a glimpse of that full life! Jesus wants to heal everyone. As the amplified translation of Acts 2:38-39 says, "[3]And Peter answered them, Repent (change your views and purpose to accept the will of God in your inner selves instead of rejecting it) and be baptized, every one of you, in the name of Jesus Christ for the forgiveness of *and* release from your sins; and you shall receive the gift of the Holy Spirit." (Did you see that? HE wants to release us from whatever holds us in bondage.)

Through my search for what's "wrong" with me, I discovered I was a "Highly Sensitive Person" (this does not mean I cry at the drop of a hat) or the trait's scientific term, Sensory-Processing Sensitivity (SPS). Dr. Elaine Aron found that it is an innate trait that is found in 15% to 20% of the population-too many to be a condition, disorder, or a diagnosis but not enough to be well understood by the majority of people.

HSPs process stimuli in a highly organized "big picture" way which includes awareness of fine distinctions and subtleties that others might not notice. All the senses (sounds, sights, touch, smell) are hyper-alert at all times and HSPs feel emotions deeper than other people. They are extremely conscientious (aware of consequences of failing to do things well). At times, HSPs can become overstimulated by the great amount of information they may be processing, thus becoming more easily overwhelmed and exhausted. They must try to arrange their lives to avoid upsetting or overwhelming situations.

This trait is not a new discovery, but it has been misunderstood. Because HSPs prefer to process things (mull things over) before entering new situations, they are often labeled "shy." But shyness is learned, not innate. In fact, 30% of HSPs are extroverts. Sensitivity is valued differently in different cultures. In cultures where it is not valued (such as United States), HSPs tend to have low self-esteem and feel abnormal. You can see why this complicated my life even more.

I included this information about HSPs because theoretically, 15% - 20% of you reading this may be questioning what is wrong with you...guess what....there is nothing wrong with you. It's just a trait you were born with. You may feel it's a hindrance, but it can be a great gift, especially a gift to humanity with your highly-tuned empathy and your creative inclination. You can learn more about it here: http://hsperson.com/

I stumbled upon a new revelation that has freed me from a lifetime of depression. Robert Henderson discovered that we can go before the Courts of Heaven to plead our case, often freeing us from past generational strongholds. I have always been in awe of Daniel 7 where Daniel saw "The court was seated, and the books were opened." So when I heard Robert Henderson speak of this, I knew it was spot on. Anyone who continually struggles with something, whether it be depression, addiction or any obstacle over and over again probably needs to ask God to reveal the root of the problem and then take it to His Courts. You can find Robert Henderson speak about this on youtube and/or on Sid Roth.

So...what ever happened to waking up in a state of terror? After realizing I was having these recurring dreams, I woke up one morning with that sick feeling and thought, "These dreams are trying to tell me something. What is it?" Suddenly, God revealed it to me...the dreams were telling me I had been sexually abused as a baby.

I had never told my mom of this realization but she just casually mentioned to me that she had to put me on a cup at six months old because I would no longer suck from a bottle. She had to take me to the doctor because I was losing weight, but I refused to drink from a bottle. (At one point, she also revealed that as a baby, I had to get shots once a week but she didn't know why [an STD perhaps?].)

Now, as an adult, I can reason out why life and people have always been so fearful for me. Besides the emotional abuse and neglect, I learned at the very beginning of my life that even my own instincts brought me something horrible...not only could I not trust people and life, I could not even trust myself!

My mother also told me I learned to use a potty chair at the age of nine months old...I crawled to it, pulled down my own diaper and used the potty chair. Now I wonder what that was all about...more to be revealed perhaps? ...perhaps the dream where I woke up running down the hall? If there is more to be revealed, I know WHO lives within me so I don't fear it!

"I made a decision that all of my abuse, my past,
and my depression was buried with him...It was God's plan."

BJYounger, OSB
2017

"But he said to me, My grace is sufficient for you, for my power is made perfect in weakness. Therefore I will boast all the more gladly of my weaknesses, so that the power of Christ may rest upon me."
2 Corinthians 12:9(ESV)

Brandee's Story

This is my fight song! Take back my life Song!!!!

I grew up on a farm in central South Dakota. We had cattle and lived in the middle of nowhere; at least for a kid that is what I thought. Neighbors were miles apart. My grandparents did live a half a mile away, and I spent as much time there as I could.

When I was young, real young, I was groomed by my oldest brother. He is 8 years older than I was. He blamed me for the things he did just to do them and get away with it. This started as early as five years old. My brothers, the other one is two years older than I, were playing catch in their upstairs room and threw the baseball into the sheetrock and made a hole. I got blamed for that one. Wow! Did I get in big trouble for that. Now let me ask you, would a typical five year old have the strength to throw a baseball hard enough and high enough to make a hole in the sheetrock? Not a tough question for many is it?

If my oldest brother wanted cookies or extra avocado or other extra treats, he would kick us under the table or pinch or punch us to have us give him ours. We weren't allowed to tell our parents. This happened right in front of our parents!

My oldest brother found out about every fear of mine and would bring them to life when babysitting, or when I was about to sleep. He would lock me in a dark closet, a dark shop, or hide under my bed or beside it. He would also scare me with clowns and scary masks causing me to stare myself to sleep, even into adulthood.

My brother wrote the year I graduated all over the mirrors in lipstick when I was five. I didn't even know what that meant. My oldest brother got so much pleasure out of treating my other brother and I like slaves. I was humiliated often. One time I had to be a human footstool for hours while my parents were away.

Then it progressed when I was about seven or eight into sexual abuse until I was somewhere between twelve or fourteen. I am not sure. He used my sensitive heart and told me my parents would send him away, and it would be all my fault if I told on him.

One time in particular, I was in the family pool. My Mom was around the yard. Both brothers came in the pool. My oldest made the other be the lookout. I started to freak out. I lied and got away and started running and screaming once I got out of the pool. My oldest brother came after me and slapped me, hard. He told me to get a handle and calm down. I was trying to defend myself, and he still took over control of me. I hated him for that. He made me get back in the pool. I could never get away from him. He was so much bigger and stronger than I. I couldn't believe Mom never knew. He made up some story about me getting scared to convince her why I was so upset.

I was about 10 years old while watching the Ten Commandments on T.V., and I freaked out and thought I was a horrible person for lying by not telling my parents. I told about the other stuff like bullying and blaming, etc., just not the sexual abuse. The abuse and bullying and blaming got worse. My oldest brother tried to separate me from my best friend and get her into trouble, so we couldn't be friends, and I would have no one to confide in. I didn't confide in her either.

My entire childhood and high school years I spent proving to my parents and myself that I was a good person and got the best grades and was involved in everything I could be involved in. I was bullied everywhere I went in grade school, high school in and out of groups. I just wanted to be friends with everyone.

My best friend lived three miles away, and she picked up that I was weaker, so she tried to toughen me up by trying to help me face my fears. I must have worn them for all to see - fear of the dark, fear of heights, scary movies, etc. She would hide in her attic closets and wait until I was nearly asleep and jump out. She would wait until we were going to bed and would shut off all the lights and run upstairs, so she could jump out of one of the rooms to scare me. She also had me climb a ladder, held it, and then left me hanging and took off on her bike. Years later when I told her, she felt terrible that she was making the situation worse and felt like a bad friend. I told her I would rather be at her house than mine.

My oldest brother got away with everything! He did all those mean things to me and blamed me so much so Mom and Dad would never believe me. That is how he controlled me to not say anything about the sexual abuse. How sick and cruel to manipulate a child! How sick and cruel to take something so precious from them. How sick and cruel to possibly ruin their life!

One morning my parents and other brother were at the Denver Stock Show and I was in high school. My oldest brother came into the locked bathroom while I was showering. I was so petrified and angry that I freaked out and started yelling and screaming and cursing. He knew there was no calming me down and left. That was the last time he ever tried anything.

I locked out the sick and scary things he did to me and had no intentions of letting it out. On my Jr. Prom night, my boyfriend and I had a little to drink. I had not had anything to drink since the summer after the eighth grade at my brother's wedding because my oldest brother told my parents I was drinking to get me into trouble; however, he was the one who gave it to me. How sick is that! I opened up and told my boyfriend everything. I had never told anyone before. He was so supportive.

I never wanted to be home by myself. I had an uncle that was touchy-feely too and tried to walk in while I was showering a few times. I always had to be on the phone when I was home alone, and he would magically appear at the farm.

My mother was quite controlling, and after I graduated I spent a lot of time at my boyfriend's house. She demanded one night for me to come home in the middle of the night; I had been gone long enough. She didn't believe my excuse of night blindness anymore. Why would she? My boyfriend begged me to tell them when I got there what happened to me. After arguing, I got this look in my eye, and he knew when I agreed to tell them just exactly what I was going to do.

I don't know how God showed him, but he knew I was going to get in my Z24 Chevy Cavalier and drive so fast once I hit the road and drive right into the pole and kill myself. He knew. So, he said, "I will go with you and be right there beside you when you tell them."

I told him, "They won't believe me."

I was greeted with two angry parents, and when they saw my boyfriend they weren't any happier. They just assumed I was going to make yet another excuse.

I won't forget the look on my dad's face, his arms crossed. My mom's too. No disbelief, no belief. I take that back, more disbelief than anything. Kind of in shock. They kindly let my boyfriend stay with me to comfort me for the night and said we would discuss it in the morning. They wanted to ask my brother in the morning if it was true! That is what they did too! He admitted to it and then nothing really happened. They just left me to fend for myself. I think my Mom said when you go to SDSU, see a counselor. That was kind of her.

I locked it away, once again. I tried the counselor for a while at SDSU that fall. It helped for a while until he tried to put thoughts in my head that my dad was an abuser too! That was not the case. My father was not the disciplinarian at all. He was my positive influence in every other aspect other than this. He just didn't know why he had to encourage me so much. He would always tell me to "keep your head up," "speak up," "Today is the first day of the rest of your life!" So you can probably predict what I am going to say next...I quit counseling.

The next few years, I was married to the same boyfriend who saved me, yet unhappy were we. He didn't show much interest in me. Not consistently. I had a couple of one night stands, not sure what I was trying to find or fulfill. He still stayed with me. He passed guilt on me and controlled me from high school all throughout our marriage. We had children and still we weren't happy. He would go to the bar all the time, and I took care of the kids. One night after work I went to the bar and had another one night stand. He demanded I go to the counseling center for help.

I had to go through alcohol classes. He wouldn't let me drink, but he wouldn't give up drinking. I had to go through counseling too. This was where I faced my sexual abuse that was buried so deep. I really liked my counselor, and he made me understand why I was looking to men to fix me. At the end of the counseling, as part of the therapy, I had to write a letter to my oldest brother. I had the choice to rip it up, keep it, give it to the counselor, or send it. I chose to send it. My brother's wife intercepted it and used it for evil! She divorced my brother and took their two kids. She also used the letter against the family for the next twelve years.

My parents complained to me about the ex-wife all the time (making me feel guilty) and the custody battle. I would try to get them to stop, and it would just upset them. One time my mother said to me, "He would never do anything, he isn't capable."

I said, "He is, he did! This is why rape victims don't say anything because no one believes them." A couple hours later, I received a call from my father yelling at me and telling me to never treat my mother like that again and that she is the most kind hearted, Christian woman around. I said, "Ok" and hung up.

I hated going to family functions. I was never my true self my entire life. I didn't know who I was. I acted just weird and different around my family. At home with my kids, I wasn't even myself. I didn't trust. I didn't have many true friends. Girls or women were so competitive, not sure why.

A couple of years ago, my brother completed his therapy, and they were nearing the horrific custody battle. He asked if I would talk to the social worker. I agreed. See. I had at some point forgiven him, and we became friends/siblings again with respect. He had apologized several times. Well, I spiraled again and became even more depressed before the call. My husband tried to support me and said he could come home from work. I answered all the questions and truly believed at the time that he was "cured" and okay. I didn't mind my kids being around him, but I wouldn't let them stay overnight.

A few months later the case worker called back to say the case was closed. She wanted to tell me she was so proud of the woman I had become. She has had a copy of my letter for years and worried about me the entire time. She couldn't believe that I have the career I do and family and marriage (still married to the same guy, in love) with what I went through. I cried and cried. To have the acknowledgment from a perfect stranger that I will never meet and not to get it from my own family, absolutely crazy. I didn't know how to handle it. I stayed depressed for two more years.

My husband of 19 years and 11 months asked me one day, "How are you doing?"

I said, "You know, pretty good. I actually don't feel like dying."

He said, "Well, you shouldn't feel that way."

Two weeks later, my husband passed away. Wow! What a shock! I made a decision that all of my abuse, my past, and my depression was buried with him. It had to be as I had three kids to raise. It wasn't my choice. It was God's plan. My brothers were both there for me through the funeral and afterwards. I told my oldest brother that all was buried, and it didn't matter anymore.

I met an amazing man with God's help, and my heavenly husband's at a concert five months later. The next year, I started getting sick with numerous things. In the summer I started having seizure-like symptoms, and I would be unresponsive and shake, yet I could hear and remember what was going on through them. Some of them lasted a half hour at a time. I was diagnosed with Psychological Conversion Disorder due to the traumas in my life.

The biggest traumas were the sexual abuse and my family's lack of support. Even to this day, my brothers won't talk to me. They never came to the hospital any of the time I was in. I tried to reach out to them. For months I wouldn't talk to my parents. They all couldn't figure out why I was bringing it up again. My disorder is my body's way of getting it out from suppressing it for so long.

I had to take a couple months off of work. I went back to work, and they placed some restrictions on me and then knocked me down to 35 hours. After eight months of returning and lots of medication, my work fired me. They couldn't wait for me to get better. There must have been too much stress and memories there because as soon as I was let go, I was better. The next day, God told me to forgive my parents, so I called my Mom, and we now have a normal relationship. We silently know we just don't talk about the abuse.

I remembered God telling me when I was little that "Good will come of this." Good has come of this. Hope in God is an amazing group and has made an amazing impact in my life and the lives of others. I meet people all the time, and we look right into each other's souls and just know, you know? So we talk about things. God is Good, God is Great, and God is Awesome!

Prove I am alright song
My power's turned on
Starting right now I'll be strong

Rachel Platten sings it well. Without God I am not able to be here today and fight through and prove I am alright.

One last thought to leave you with is another song as music has gotten me through my life's journey along with God holding my hand.

"Brave" by Sara Bareilles
You can be amazing
You can start speaking up
You say what you want to say
Honestly, I want to see you be Brave

We are all in this together in this journey. We don't have to do this alone. We are not alone. He is ALWAYS with us.

"He apologized for hurting me...
I just stayed there with my cousin
until she woke up."

"Record my misery; list my tears on your scroll - are they not in your record?"

Psalm 56:8

Shay's Story

When I was the age of thirteen, I lost my dad. I had a hard time dealing with his death. My family fell apart. My mother, brother and I grieved his death. When I turned fourteen, my mother just up and left us. She was gone for two weeks. She was on a binge. We didn't know where she was. We didn't know when or if she was going to come home. During this time, I took care of my brother. Every day, I took care of my brother. I fed him. Got him ready for school and made sure that he was okay—even though he was a "pain." Previously, dad and mom told my brother and I, "One day, it would just be the two of you." With dad's death and mom abandoning us, it was so true.

I made sure that my brother ate, but eventually, our cabinets became bare and empty. I checked with my dad's side of the family, but they didn't have any food for him. My heart was heavy. I packed our belongings into two duffle bags. One duffle bag was mine and the other was my brother's. We walked to my grandmother's house. I cried. I knew there wasn't enough room for both of us. I asked my grandmother if my brother could stay with her because he needed her more than I did. I knew that I could stay with friends. I thought I could check on him from time to time and that my grandmother would take care of him. Then, I left him there to go find my own place, if someone would take me in.

My friend, Jesse had lost his father the same year I lost my dad. One day, Jesse and I went to Sara's place. We were partying and drinking. Jesse was quiet. I thought I knew how he felt—just trying to get through the day. He loved his father so much and losing him was hard. I'm very compassionate and so I wanted to help him. I told Jesse that my heart went out to him and that I was willing to sit and listen to him. My heart went out to him and I told him that I could talk to him for a while, if that helped. The music, laughter and conversation were loud inside of the house. Jesse asked me to go outside with him so that we could talk. So, we went outside. I had known Jesse for a while. I thought we were family. I thought he was a friend. I felt safe with him. So, I went outside with him. He talked me into going behind the house because he didn't want anyone to see him crying. I understood. Almost every day I fought my tears. I didn't want anyone to know how much I hurt. Our talk went well. He thanked me and asked me for a hug. I gave him a hug, but when I tried to pull away he hugged me tighter. Then, Jesse tried to kiss me. I tried to push him away. I tried to "play it off" and said things like, "Dang Dude, you're drunk. Ok? Hang in there, cuz." I felt unsafe but didn't know what to do. I didn't scream or yell for help or kick or hit him. I just thought—he's drunk. I laughed nervously and got out of his tight grip. Slowly, calmly, I walked away. Then, Jesse grabbed me, again. I said, "No. Stop it." I told him that he was hurting me and to let me go. Then, I thought—maybe I just play along so that I can get him to stop hurting me. He didn't listen to me. I thought—if I can just get away, I'll keep my distance from him. So, I allowed him to kiss me. It worked and he let me go, momentarily. Then, Jesse grabbed me again—this time, tighter. He pulled and pushed me down. After that, things got hazy. I was so scared "my mind just broke up into bits." I remember yelling and screaming. I told him to stop. I prayed that someone would hear me. I thought, someone will come and look for me. Someone will wonder where I am. I remember kicking and hitting or something. Finally, he got off me. So, I ran. I tried to run inside of the house but he stood in front of me. Even though he was drunk, he was fast and he was strong. So, I ran for the fields, thinking that I could make it to the store. After all, I had played basketball since the 3rd grade. I ran as hard and fast as I could. My legs hurt. I kept screaming and crying because each time I looked over my shoulder, Jesse was chasing me.

I thought to myself—things like this don't happen here. It happens in other places, like big cities, but not here on our little "rez." Then, I could see the store. I was getting closer and closer. I thought to myself, "I am going to make it." Then, boom! I fell to the ground. I didn't trip or anything. Then, I realized that he hit me. He caught me. He knocked me to the ground. I screamed and cried until my voice cracked. He rolled me over onto my back. I cried, I kicked. I screamed, I begged him to stop. He hit me in the side of my head. I thought, "This is it." I closed my eyes. I tried to escape. I didn't want to see. I didn't want to remember.

The next time I know...I hear people saying, "What are you doing? Shay, are you okay? Come on." I feel two people pulling me up by my arms. I was scared. I tried to pull away. Then, I realized it was my friends saying, "Come on, Shay…it's okay." They walked me to the house. My legs "felt like Jell-O." So, I leaned on them for support. My feet were dragging. All my energy and all my fight were gone—it took everything within me just to survive. I kept telling myself, "It's okay. It's going to be okay."

When we got inside the house, they helped me to a bed. I cried hard sobs until it hurt to breathe. My friend, Sara pulled the weeds and dirt from my hair and clothes. She told me, "It's okay, Shay." She gave me something to drink. Then, someone said, "Shay, someone's here for you." My cousin, Casey arrived. I remember looking up at him and he just hugged me. I didn't respond because I didn't have the energy to hug him back. I was numb. He asked me what happened and I shrugged my shoulders. He asked me if Jesse hurt me. I nodded, "Yes." Casey said, "Jesse stopped at the house and was saying something happened, so I grabbed my bike and came over right away to check on you, but he shouldn't have done that."

Then, my aunts arrived at the house. They said to me, "Get your butt in the car." I did. I didn't even say goodbye to my friends. I just got into the car. My aunts looked at me and never asked me what happened. They just "passed me a doob." I smoked it and welcomed the haze that came over me. My aunts took me to my grandmother's place in central housing. The alcohol and weed did nothing to calm me down. I was still so scared. I walked into my aunt's room to tell her what Jesse did to me. I cried. She looked at me and said, "Oh well. No biz going out and drinking. Oh, bullshit. You probably wanted it. Well, that what you get." Her words hurt me so deeply. I didn't ask for that to happen to me. I walked out of my aunt's room and into a room I was sharing with my younger cousin, James. He asked me what happened. I didn't say anything. I laid down on the bed and curled into a ball. James didn't say anything. He just rubbed my back and I cried myself to sleep.

The next morning, I took a shower. I still felt like Jesse was "on me." I could still feel the dirt and weeds in my hair and on me. I scrubbed and washed myself like never before. I brushed my hair and changed my clothes again and again. I wanted to forget. Finally, I went downstairs and had coffee with my grandma. My mom was there. She asked me what had happened. I told her, "I was almost raped." She said nothing. Then, I excused myself because the school bus was outside waiting for me. I kept telling myself, "Okay, okay. It's going to be okay."

I walked into the High School and right into Jesse and his friends who were standing around him in the entryway. Jesse laughed at me and said, "You wanted it." I wanted to scream, "No, you're wrong. How could you do that to me? How could you do that to me, your cousin?" I was too afraid to speak. All I could do was run. Every day, I ran into him and it was the same thing over again. I tried to forget it. I tried to hide it. Then one day, I told Jesse to stay away from me. He and his friends just laughed at me.

Finally, I told the school counselors. I was crying when I opened the door to their office. It like I could barely breathe. I stood in her doorway and I told her what had happened and what was going on. She just looked at me and said, "You need treatment." I ran out of her office. Jesse was right. No one cared about what he did to me. No one believed me.

I called my mom and grandma. I begged them to come and get me. I told them that I couldn't go to school. I just couldn't do it. I didn't feel well. I repeated this behavior for a week. Then, one day, an officer came to the school and talked to me. I told him and another officer what Jesse did to me.

Afterwards, I ran into Jesse's mom. She yelled and cussed at me. I just walked away crying and thinking to myself, "I can't do this anymore." I thought about ending my life. But I had dreams and things deep down inside of me—and a voice that kept telling me, "I did nothing wrong. It wasn't my fault." I knew I couldn't go to "Fort" or Crow Creek anymore, so, I decided to change schools and went to Lower Brule.

I found comfort knowing that no one knew me. My father went to Lower Brule. I could follow in his footsteps. For a while, I felt free. I was only there for one quarter. That voice was still inside of me and it got louder and louder. It told me that what Jesse did to me was wrong. I got mad. I knew that I did nothing wrong. I thought to myself, "Why should I be the one to leave?" I decided to go home and to be strong. I decided to face him. So, I re-enrolled at Crow Creek. However, I never ran back into Jesse. So, I just went to school and lived my life. Some years later, I ran into him at the store. The fear came back and I wanted to bolt and run. I put items I had in my hand back on the shelves and left the store empty-handed. All the way home, I kept thinking, "No! Don't allow him to have this power over you. You did nothing wrong."

Some time has passed by and I received a call from my cousin who asked me to come and get her. She was at a party at Jesse's house. When I arrived, she was passed out on the couch. I tried to move her but she was completely passed out. I couldn't leave her because I knew what would happen to her. I tried to get her up but couldn't. So, I just lied down on the couch with her. I wanted to protect her. Then, Jesse came into the room where we were. Fear rose in me. He said, "Hi, like nothing ever happened." I anticipated him saying snide remarks and disgusting jokes as he did in high school—but Jesse said nothing of the sort. Instead, Jesse told me that she'd be fine sleeping there. He offered to help me get her up. I told him that he was not going to touch her. I told him to stay away from her. During the encounter, Jesse must have remembered me. He got quiet. Then, Jesse totally surprised me. He apologized for hurting me and said that he will never do that to anyone, again. I wanted to scream...to cry. I just begged him to not touch us. He said, "Okay." He left us and went back into the room from which he came. So, I just stayed there with my cousin until she woke up. Then, we left Jesse's house.

I left his house that morning feeling like the nightmare was over. I didn't let him destroy me. Despite the blame and hurt that came from people that didn't believe me. I am a survivor of sexual assault—I'm ready to stand up for others and willing to share my story in hopes it encourages others to break their silence about sexual abuse and assault. It's kept too many of us silent for too long.

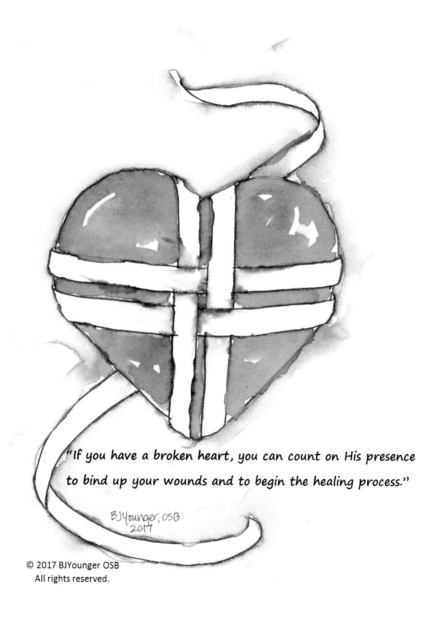

"If you have a broken heart, you can count on His presence to bind up your wounds and to begin the healing process."

BJYounger, OSB
2017

"He heals the brokenhearted and binds up their wounds."

Psalm 147:3

Jenn's Story

In early spring of 1997, Watertown, South Dakota, my hometown, was facing one of the biggest floods known to the community. It engulfed homes. The flood waters forced countless families out of their homes. In the tragedy of it all, the community came together. They began filling and placing sandbags to prevent the rising waters from reaching more homes and businesses. Countless times people wanted to give up, let the waters in because simply, it was easier.

I envision my childhood much like a home surrounded by the water. There is nothing able to be saved by the way it looks. Help can be standing twenty feet on the solid ground outside but unable to reach me. It appears as though whoever was in the home at the time the flood waters rose was able to get to safety. They never thought to investigate further. If they had, they would have found and helped me. The waters just kept coming in. There was no stopping them. My emotions were locked inside, and there was no way to reach them. The water rose higher and faster. Before I knew it, my emotions and childhood were trapped. I worked tirelessly filling sandbags, reaching my hand out for someone to come help me. It was too late. The havoc-destruction-devastation caused by this flood was the same destructiveness I experienced growing up being sexually abused as a child, and I know many other survivors have gone through trials similar to mine.

I am an incest survivor. I continue to heal each and every day with the help of God, my family, friends, and the amazing advocates I have come to know.

I don't recall all of the details, but I do remember before I was in grade school another older female cousin of mine would have me perform oral penetration on her. I remember I did not like the smell, or the taste. It felt as though I had to go through with it though, or she would tell on me, and I did not want to get into trouble. This occurred at least a dozen times. It was always at her house, never mine.

I was next abused by my brother. I was in the third grade. It may have started before this, but this is the earliest memory I have. I was so unsure of what was happening. All I knew is I wanted him to love me, not beat on me as the sexual and physical abuse was something normal for him to do almost daily. He blamed me for the abuse.

I remember telling my "big sister" from the Big Brothers, Big Sisters program I was involved in through the Boys and Girls Club. She then turned it in to authorities. They came to my school and talked to me, pulled my mom out of work and talked to her. At home later that night I sat atop the steps while my parents questioned my brother, and frequently I heard him saying, "She made me do it." I felt ashamed....I felt dirty....I felt sick...I felt as though I had been thrown down into a hole dug six feet deep, dirt and rocks hurled at me as I lay there crying out tears, but no one could see or hear me....I was too far away. He touched my privates...he groped me in the middle of the night...I prayed this was the end....boy was I wrong. I felt as though God didn't love me, that he failed and left me. I was all alone.

For a very long time I blamed my parents for allowing the abuse to continue even after it was brought to the attention of the authorities. It felt as though they chose a side in all of it, and I wasn't worthy of being fought for or believed. I felt like the dirty, torn apart shop rag thrown into the corner waiting for someone to sweep it up into the trash. How was I not better than the rag in the trash?

My cousin/best friend was also abused by my brother. She and I are the same age. Thankfully, she was practically one of the only people who believed the abuse happened and continued to happen. When I would try to express concern to others about leaving their daughters alone with him, I would get told, "Oh stop. You are just holding a grudge. He is a big teddy bear." This made me so angry. I prayed he did not ever steal any other person's innocence the way he stole mine. My heart hurts deeply to admit, but this also led to her and me engaging in oral penetration on each other. I believe there were sometimes we also physically penetrated each other. I always excused this away as we were comforting each other. I know it doesn't excuse or make any of it right, but it is how I rationalized things in my mind.

She was afraid to spend the night with me because my brother would abuse her. I wanted her to stay over, so I could avoid being victimized for once. I carried around so much guilt and shame for this. It progressed from there....eventually to him performing oral sex...and penetration. I dreaded sleeping. His abuse didn't just progress for me, but for my cousin as well. Even though we both were going through Hell, neither of us spoke of what had happened. We were both the youngest of our families and did not want to cause trouble for anyone, so we kept this heavy-boulder-mountain of a secret to ourselves. I came to despise my brother from whom I should have felt love and protection. I couldn't call out for help...no one would believe me...or hear me anyway.

I remember a time there were many of us gathered at my grandparents' house. It must have been some sort of holiday. The adults were in the kitchen and dining room. The kids were supposed to be asleep in the living room. An older male cousin of mine climbed on top of me and began kissing the back of my neck. It sent shivers down my spine. I did not call out for help. I guess by this time, I assumed no one would believe or help me. Then he began moving in an upward and downward motion on top of my body. He whispered to me, "Do you like this?" I cringed and shook my head in agreement.

It has recently been brought to my attention that my brother and another male cousin of mine would take their turns with me. They both penetrated me. I did not recall this whatsoever. Until a month or two after learning about the experience, the images began playing in my mind. I did my best to shut them out. How does one do that? I could see them both standing there. One would finish and motion for the other to come have his way with me. I was maybe 12 or 13 years old. Then when they were finished, they would talk and brag about it. I would get up and get dressed as quickly as I could.

What I found to be the hardest to deal with to date are two things. One is admitting it was incest. How could any member of my own family do this to me? It would be so much easier to tell people if it was just regular sexual abuse. I cannot be the one to tear my family apart. The second thing is coming to terms with the fact that yes, the body naturally responds to sexual conduct. Because of this, there were times I would initiate the sexual contact. It is completely normal for a body to respond to sexual stimulation. The other reason I would initiate the contact was to just get it over and done with. These two things have had my brain so messed up. What is wrong with me? Why on earth would I want my brother or my cousin to have sex with me? Maybe you have had these thoughts flooding through your mind. They are lies, lies straight from the Devil. He wants you to believe that you are dirty, you are worthless. None of these things are true. It took me a long time to accept that I am not in the wrong.

I moved out when I was 14 into another cousin's house to help her with her kids....just to feel safe. I did not escape abuse there either. The male cousin who would take his turn with me would come to visit often and spend the night quite a bit. We had this weird relationship where sometimes it felt as though we were dating. The sexual encounters happened more and more frequently. Again I find myself questioning how or why I could be doing these things. The answer I have found is the abuse I had endured in my life had skewed my view on how relationships and love were supposed to be.

The sexual torture as I recall it continued on until my brother went to college out of state when I was 15 or 16. I sensed relief with him gone. I was home much more. The time came when he finished college and got divorced. He ended up moving home. The fear and dread of being home washed over me all over again. One night, I had my door locked...I woke up to hearing my door opening...sudden terror streamed over my body...I was frozen in fear. He came in a few minutes later. I kicked him away, and he left. He would try grabbing my butt as I was passing by. It felt as though I was being pushed down by the waves of the ocean, unable to come up for breath. I was sinking further and further into the deep dark pit of the ocean. I am unsure how I would free myself. I ended up letting my emotions and part of my identity go just to be able to come up for air. I was in a long distance relationship at the time....I made the choice to move away....to get away....I just couldn't allow it to happen anymore. My freedom came at a high cost though.

I went through my college years lost and confused about who I was. I thought I loved others with my whole heart, but I didn't. I robbed them of knowing who I truly was. God was not a part of my life. After I prayed faithfully for Him to save me from the abuse and it continued happening, I ran far away from God without looking back. I threw myself into college. I finished a semester early, moved back to my hometown, and found myself an apartment. This was when I really began self-sabotaging. I went to the local bars regularly. I slept with men whom I knew had no interest in me. I threw myself at almost anybody that would have me. I used drugs, sex, and alcohol to numb the feelings even more. I didn't want to remember my past. There were times people would question me whether it happened, and I denied it. I got so tired of trying to prove myself to be right.

I started working a good job living in a new town with my grandmother. I went back home for the weekend knowing my parents were out of town for the weekend. I told myself I didn't plan to go to the bar one particular night. I think I really wanted to go. It was this night that God began moving in my life. He brought this man into my life. I was still not looking for Him as I attempted to use this man as a one night stand, but he saw and wanted more than that. We began dating shortly after that weekend. We moved in together, got pregnant, and married all in less than a year of knowing each other. Yes, many people can claim I was just throwing myself into this to avoid the feelings more. That is partly true.

Now being married, I find myself having difficulty with sex and pleasure. I do not know how to allow myself to see myself how God sees me. I don't know how to allow myself to feel pleasure. God has granted us with four beautiful children. My brother is no longer a part of our lives as he chooses to deny any responsibility and not deal with it. I also do not trust him around my children, not only my daughters but my sons as well. I am unsure the extent in which his abuse reaches for certain.

My abuse has played a profound role in my adult and married life. I fear I am not able to be there and give my husband the things he needs sexually, and for that I question whether or not to stay, but I do because of the kids. There have been times I have started regretting my life... my marriage... my kids... everything. I came to a very dark place in my life in October of 2014. I started to make a plan to end my own life. It is still hard for me to grasp the idea. I was so far down and felt unreachable, but God really made himself known to me through the K-LOVE app. There were several people who reached out to me. Somehow, through these people, they prayed faithfully for me and with me. As I sat in the bathtub one evening crying, I poured my heart out to my husband. I confessed the fact I counted some of my medication and searched how many it would take to end my life. He looked me straight in the eyes and asked if he needed to get me help. I sat for a few minutes thinking and then calmly responded, "No. God has this. He has me. I will be okay." And I was. He brought me up out of the dark pit I was trapped in.

I truly believe that I went through my abuse for a reason....one of which I have not yet been shown. I have survived thus far and know that God wants to create a new me. "Therefore, if anyone is in Christ, he is a new creation. The old has passed away; behold, the new has come," from 2 Corinthians 5:17. I never thought this applied to me. I am not worth this kind of love. But, allowing myself to give control to God and allow Him to work in my life has begun to open my eyes to new outlets of healing. As I continue sharing my story and reaching out to others, my healing changes day by day. I am renewed always. It is not just a one-time thing for me. He is constantly changing and renewing my soul.

When we feel so deep in despair-destruction-devastation, we feel as though we are crushed. We are unlovable. We feel broken and shattered. When David wrote this, he wrote it directly to me it seems. I felt all of this. Psalms 34:18 states, "The Lord is near to the brokenhearted and saves those who are crushed in spirit." A devotion I read on this verse stated, "The word 'broken' in Hebrew is the word 'shabar' and means 'to rend violently or crush; to maim, cripple or break.' 'Shabar' was used to describe ships that had been splintered and torn due to ferocious and wild winds. It was also used to describe the tearing and ripping that wild, ravenous beasts performed upon their prey. When the psalmist declares (this), he is reminding us that the Lord is lovingly attentive to those who are enduring unimaginable pain. If you are emotionally torn apart and wonder how you will make it through one more today, be comforted with the surety that He is with you. If you have a broken heart, you can count on His presence to bind up your wounds and to begin the healing process. Do not push Him away at these moments but welcome Him and receive His comfort. Many Christians squeeze God out of their lives at the very time they need Him most desperately. I know I definitely did! No one will comfort you like the Lord. Jesus has taken all of the things that have broken your heart to the cross of Calvary. He wanted you to live an abundant life on earth! The pain has already been carried and has been laid at the foot of the cross. (Declare) 'God is close to me. When my life is falling apart I will draw near to the One who is able to comfort me."

In October of 2016, I made a choice to truly start my healing. Yes, God had been doing small things here and there, but I felt called to take this to the next level. I searched and searched to find a facility for treatment. I have PTSD, Bipolar type 2, and some insomnia. I found a facility located outside of Seattle, WA. That is 1700 miles from my husband, children, and family. My husband supported me 100% of the way. He wanted this for me more than I did sometimes. Thankfully, he never let me quit and pushed me onward. I went to The Center-A Place of Hope in Edmonds, Washington. It was there I started to find God in my ruins. He showed himself in the staff, in the community, and in my housemates. I finally was able to identify and feel some of my emotions. I even found out I lumped my emotions into what I call "my blob." Someday, I will write a story about that. I choose not to allow my diagnosis to define who I am. Do I still struggle with them? You bet I do! I keep looking for God and giving Him the glory in all of my triumphs and trials as well. He is not only there for me in the good times, but he is hurting with me in the bad as well. I now know He was there with me as I was being abused. He felt every single thing I did. His heart broke each time.

Someone once said to me, "Seek God! Seek God recklessly! Seek God with no regard for anything but Him and His will for you! Life won't always be easy, but after the things that you have survived, as true emotions begin to flood your heart and mind, you are going to be so joyful you won't know how to express it! And I will be celebrating with you! I claim it now in Jesus' name!" And I claim this for you as well! My abuse does not define me. I now choose to let it strengthen me. I choose to let my story be heard to help others know they are not alone, to know they have a voice too, and hopefully to help them seek healing through Christ as he is our ultimate healer. I would not be able to tell my story if it weren't for Him and the people he has placed in my life.

"As the girls lifted the lanterns with us, they followed them until they got so high they looked like floating stars...I tried to remember the last time I was that innocent..."

"The people living in darkness have seen a great light; on those living in the land of the shadow of death, a light has dawned."

Matthew 4:16(NIV)

Rena's Story

My story is hard for me to tell. It brings tears to my eyes, and anger fills my heart. No matter the cost or the discomfort it may cause me or even those who will read it, it still needs to be told. I decided to write my "Monster" a letter. He needs to know what he did to me. Whether he will ever read it or not isn't important. It's that I have the strength to say the words out loud.

To the Monster under my bed,

You would come out of the darkness when no one was around. Pitch black and eyes as red as the flames from the hell you came from. Your cold fingers tearing at my soft and innocent skin. Your tongue burned my flesh as it ran across every private area of my body destroying whatever ounces of purity I had. You were shameless and unforgiving. You told me we would always have these secret moments that I would never or could ever forget. I belonged to you, and nothing would ever change that. The harder I would fight, the more you enjoyed it. I was a toy to you, one you could play with, break and put back together only to break again. When I would ask why? You would say, "Simply because I can." I would gasp for air, my throat closing shut, the lights of my world fading around me. Am I dead? Was I that bad of a little girl that all I deserved was this darkness? Will my mommy and daddy miss me, or will they even know that I'm gone? So many questions without any answers. I would scream out with my tiny little voice, "Is there any one here? Please, someone find me. I'm afraid of the dark! Please, someone come and take me home." The light finally came. I did tell on you,

Monster! But my mommy didn't believe me. If she did, she never told me so. She didn't even tell my daddy. If she had, he would have killed you, Monster under my bed! When you said, "No one will believe you," you were right because no one did. I can still hear your acidic laughter in my head. You had left me shattered. My innocent mind, body and soul were gone. I was a little girl, I trusted you. I didn't understand, but I knew I hated you for it. We were family. Family doesn't hurt each other like that. We are supposed to protect each other! I have always wondered if someone hurt you like you hurt me when you were little, or maybe you really are just a monster. It has been almost thirty years since then, but I'm not that little girl anymore. I no longer fear you; I no longer fear the dark. I am standing in the bright, amazing warmth of God's light. You said I could never win the fight between us, but I have defeated you. You have no power over me anymore!

Sincerely,
The fighter you turned me into

Now that my letter is written and the words and emotions are finally out, I am no longer afraid. My voice is being heard, and with every word I become stronger than I was before.

Recently, I was listening to a testimony with a support group of other women just like me. During this time tears flowed like booze at a bartenders' convention. We were able to be weak in the ways that we needed to be. We listened to the stories of others as well; for some, it brought back the pain, and for others it reminded us of the strength we needed to get through our darkest hours. During the testimony I was reminded of the words in Psalm 23. For the longest time I believed it was only read at funerals or in moments of sadness. During that gathering something else clicked in my head; the words themselves are not about sadness or even relating to death. Instead, they enlist strength to fight our battles, courage to face our demons, and reminders to make sure we know that we are never truly alone.

The older I get, the closer my relationship has grown with God. As a child I was taught that God's rules were the only ones that mattered, that to question even the simplest of God's rules was a sin. As small children we are more afraid of going to hell then actually trying to understand what hell really is. Here is a reality check, folks. It's not just some over exaggerated place beneath our feet filled with the burning souls of evil ruled by some half man/half beast with red skin, horns, a forked tongue and a tail. We each have our own hell. Abuse in and of itself is a Living Hell. Our dreams are real. They consume our thoughts, souls and bodies. We fight our battles 24/7. Some we lose, and others we defeat in triumph. Even when I would win one battle, another would start.

For me the seconds of my abuse turned to minutes, then the minutes turned to hours, the hours into days and finally, the days into years. As a child, I remember my emotions running from one extreme to the other. I had no clue how to control them much less explain what they were. I was given every behavioral label in the book. As a teenager, I was no longer afraid of any punishments I might have received for bad behavior. I was too busy fighting for my sanity to actually care if I got grounded or had one of the very few luxuries I did have taken away. We all can agree that as teenagers our hormones are as predictable as a bull coming out of a shoot at the rodeo. At times we act like wild animals on nights with a full moon. At fifteen I began having sex with my then boyfriend, who incidentally broke my heart three months later. At the time I never would have guessed that I could actually enjoy something that I had thought was so evil. It turns out I loved it, all of it! It became like a game to me - the higher the risk the greater the reward. After my breakup with that one, I found another boy, surprisingly enough at church who would play my game of Russian Roulette with me. I would go to unsupervised parties to get drunk or high. Neither option was more preferable over the other- just as long as I got to be free for a short time. My releases of choice were cherry vodka, weed, and sometimes even acid. I never went without punishment from those nights; the mornings after were the worst, but I never complained about my own self inflicting pain because they were all well worth it.

A few years later at the age of seventeen, I became a mom. Just three short months after that, a very important person in my life died. I remember standing in my living room the morning after it happened holding my sweet baby in my arms and thinking that I never felt more alone. As the years in my life progressed, along came more abuse, another child, abandonment from the father of my children, and a drug overdose that landed me in a mental institution where I was given a steady supply of Xanax and some other drug I can't remember the name of. For a couple more years I lived in a foggy haze some would call a life.

Because of that haze, I have very few precious memories of my children in the younger years. My illness took me to the brink of life or death. Because of my illness, I wasn't able to work or have my own place to live. I then lost custody of my children, and that feeling of loneliness I had after my loved one died was nothing compared to the gut wrenching, head spinning, heart-ripped-out-of-my-chest kind of feeling I had when I lost my children. In my eyes I had failed; I had failed my children. I wasn't who they needed me to be. After that my life went to hell in a hand-basket. I reverted back to my teenage behaviors when my children were not around. I had more coyote ugly mornings than I will ever admit to. The lowest point of my life came on a Sunday morning after I was denied a visit with my children. I found myself sitting on my kitchen floor with a bottle of Jose in one hand and a bottle of pills in the other. I was debating which I would take first when I looked up from the floor. I could see a picture of my babies hanging on my living room wall, and in that split second I knew that I couldn't take my own life without destroying theirs in the process. I pulled myself up onto the sink, opened both bottles and poured them down the drain. I began to pray with every ounce of strength I had in me. I begged for forgiveness and told God that if he would get me through this, I would never take drugs for the sole purpose of killing my emotional pain again.

More than ten years later, I can honestly say I have kept my promise. The drinking took a little bit longer to kick, but I did that too! When I would talk to my grandma (a beautiful, strong Christian woman) about my relationship with God, I would always describe it as a marriage, and just like any marriage we would have our ups and downs. When I didn't think he was listening to me or didn't give me the answer I wanted, I would just tell him he could sleep on the couch. Her response was always the same, "You know it doesn't always work like that. A couple should never go to bed angry with each other because eventually that couch will just cause a pain in the neck and make him listen less then what he already did." I wasn't married at the time, so I didn't take much stock in her advice, but let me tell you now that I am married, I can say she was telling me the God's honest truth.

My life now that I am settled down and married to a truly amazing man that I couldn't imagine my life without still isn't perfect by any means; sometimes we argue a little too meanly for our own good, but we still sleep in the same bed, always kiss each other good night and say "I Love You" before we go to sleep.

When I had my sons, I was determined to raise them to be true men. The kind they themselves can be proud of when they look in the mirror - to love with all their hearts, to be comfortable being weak when they need to be, to never raise their hands to a woman or cause her any pain, to always work hard to get what they wanted, to be well educated, to always offer a helping hand even if there is no money involved, to always respect their elders, and most importantly to know that I would always love them more than they could ever love me. Something else that I have taught my children is that if they ever break the law, they will own up to their actions like adults, and that they had better pray to God that the cops get to them before I do; otherwise, I will be in the cell next to them for beating their butts from one side of the state to the other (Sorry. I digressed).

One of my next largest fears came when we found out we were being blessed with a little girl - sounds a little strange, doesn't it? She is perfectly imperfect, beautiful and strong willed. She is everything that I like to think that I was. Having a daughter and being a survivor of sexual assault, I find myself somewhat over protective of her. In public she isn't allowed out of my or her father's sight. If it is just the two of them at a store and she has to use the bathroom, her daddy will stand guard at the door like a pit bull in a spiked collar. My fears have rubbed off on her, and she is terrified of anything or anyone she doesn't know won't hurt her. It feels like I can never let my guard down with her. Even at home when she is riding her bike in front of our house, I always have to be able to see her.

I decided to take her with me to a survivors retreat; we released lanterns into the night sky on top of a beautiful hill. That night there was another mother and daughter who were attending as well. The girls were inseparable. Their excitement for the event was beyond compare. As the girls lifted the lanterns with us, they followed them until they got so high in the sky that they looked like floating stars just close enough for us to touch. Once the lanterns were far enough away, the girls began to chase each other around the field we were in; the only light we had was from a nearby church and the full moon. I felt so relaxed and comfortable without fearing for my daughter's safety that I was able to just let her be a normal little girl. One of the greatest memories that I will always have is of that weekend, watching the girls run all over chasing each other, seeing the beautiful smiles on their faces and hearing the sweetest sounds of their laughter ring out into the once quiet night. While standing there watching them, I tried to remember the last time I was that innocent, and I painfully can't.

When thinking about my past choices, I realized that I was like a hamster on its little running wheels. I would just keep running but yet never getting anywhere. I was just too stupid to get off. When I finally did get off, I'm sure I looked like a gizmo with a glitch, hopping and twisting all over the place with no real direction or control. When I was able to get control of myself, I was finally able to focus on the things that were important to me.

In 2013, I was ready to be baptized. I told my grandpa (retired preacher) that I didn't care where we did it, and I would be happy to do it in the horse's water trough. If the muddy waters of the river Jordan could cleanse Jesus, the trough was good enough for me (he decided to turn that idea down). That day at the church he lowered me into the cool waters of the baptismal pool, and I could feel all of my pains and worries being washed away. For the few seconds I was under the water, I could sense the Lord's arms around me. I was almost saddened when he pulled me back up. When I arose and looked up at my grandpa, I could see more pride in his eyes then I had seen the day I graduated high school. As I looked out into the crowd of my family, I could see tears and smiles on the faces of everyone there. Once the praising and thanking of God were done, my grandma surprised us all with yelling out (I had never heard her raise her voice that loud before), "Throw in the soap just to get extra clean!" The church was filled with the roar of laughter.

I can now say that with age comes wisdom, and those that know me have learned that I don't have the greatest filter between my brain and mouth. I don't say sorry for it very often. I simply say, "My filter is so full of buckshot that it's hit or miss with me." I have been able to catch myself from saying something that could be offensive by praying to Jesus and asking him to wrap one arm around my shoulders and to put his other hand over my mouth. It actually works! So now that part of my story is told, I can find comfort in helping others to heal. I will promise to continue to help others heal and to be their voice of comfort in their dark times.

"You were given this life because you were strong enough to live it." -Author unknown

"I remember kneeling in the snow...
I felt an overwhelming sense of peace, love and security...
Later I learned it had been the Holy spirit that was filling me up and
giving me strength for what I knew I had to do next."

"The Lord will guide you always;
   he will satisfy your needs in a sun-scorched land
   and will strengthen your frame.
You will be like a well-watered garden,
   like a spring whose waters never fail."
                    Isaiah 58:11(NIV)

Joey's Story

My grandma gave me the nickname Joey. Apparently, I was supposed to be born a boy. So Justin became Justina, and as Grandma put it, I was "hell on wheels," so Grandma took my middle name Jo and started calling me Joey, and it stuck.

The winter of '83 was a particularly brutal one for South Dakota. As a tom-boyish seven-year-old, I remember walking on snowdrifts as high as the first story of our ramshackle house.

I remember Mommy had a can of Coca-Cola in the cupboard in the kitchen that winter where our wood burning stove couldn't keep up, and the can of cola froze so hard it exploded. Our pet goats also froze to death that winter. (If the cold didn't bother us in the winter, the roaches in our house sure did in the summer.) I recall the shame of being dirty and having others looking at my sisters and me with pity. I hated that feeling.

I loved my parents dearly but knew from an early age that Mommy wasn't right-in-the-head. At least that's what Daddy said. When I was older, I learned she suffered from severe and persistent mental illness that my father tried to beat out of her.

Both of my parents were alcoholics and had a hard time coping which resulted in my two sisters and me being neglected - seems Mommy and Daddy were always able to get beer and cigarettes though. My grandparents did the best they could trying to clean and feed us whenever we would visit them just to send us home to be neglected again.

A few days after Christmas in 1983, the pipes in our house froze and left us with no running water. Daddy was raging mad and sent me outside with a large roasting pan to collect snow, so we could melt it.

I remember kneeling in the snow and looking up at the clear, bright, star-filled sky. The moon was reflecting off the snow, and it appeared like diamonds were sparkling all around me. In the quiet night, I felt an overwhelming sense of peace, love and security. I knew in my heart everything was going to be okay. Later I learned it had been the Holy Spirit that was filling me up and giving me strength for what I knew I had to do next.

After bringing the pan of snow back in the house, my daddy sent me to bed with no supper because I couldn't fix a cupboard he had broken which was fine because we didn't have any food anyway. We didn't have a phone either, so there was no calling for help.

Daddy yelled at Mommy that he was going to the bar, and we'd better have the house cleaned and fixed up by the time he got back, or there would be "hell to pay." Daddy slammed the door and drove off down the deserted gravel road.

I knew in my very core that tonight was different and that when Daddy came back, it could likely be the end - worse than the shovel incident where he struck Mommy over the head and blood was running down her face, worse than the butcher knife incident where he burned all of Mommy's clothes and chased her out of the house naked with me running after her to protect her naked body while I knocked on the neighbor's door to ask for help and even worse than the gun incident where after Daddy had raped Mommy in front of us girls, he shot a hole in the wall right above Mommy's head as she lay crying on their bed.

On this December night, I took Mommy aside and told her in no uncertain terms we needed to leave now. Tonight.

All of us were terrified. My sisters and I got on our threadbare coats, gave Mommy the half dollar pieces Grandma had given us for Christmas, and headed out walking down the icy road. We walked for a mile ducking and hiding whenever we saw headlights.

Finally, we made it to my teacher's house where I knew we would be safe and warm. My teacher's husband drove us to the nearest city's police department where we had to say good-bye to Mommy. The State of South Dakota put us into emergency foster care once again. This time ended up being different though because after a couple weeks we were put into permanent foster care with a family in rural South Dakota. All parental rights were eventually terminated, and my sisters and I became wards of the State.

On a farm in foster care, I learned about hard work while doing chores, loneliness while being in limbo with no parents or friends to confide in or trust, and fear from a foster brother who was ten years older than I.

The very first time he looked at me I sensed I was in trouble. I was seven, and he looked at me with a sly smile. I felt like I was his prey, and my stomach dropped as I turned away from him.

I kept my distance the best I could but observed my older sister began acting out with lies, attempts at running away and hoarding food.

At night I would lay awake and thought I saw his shadow in my sister's bed but convinced myself it was just a bad dream until I was left alone with him, and he first started with rubbing against me, then touching me and then escalating to raping me.

I could not believe I had been taken from one scary dysfunctional house and put into another one. Why? Where was God?

A year-and-a-half went by until my sisters and I were adopted, but by the Grace of God we were adopted all together (despite my foster brother routinely telling us nobody would ever adopt us, and we would be separated.) We were considered a special needs adoption because we were older and a sibling group. My older sister was ten, I was nine, and my little sister was six when we went to go live with our new parents. My sisters and I never talked about what happened to us, and we tried to put the past behind us. However, until you do the work, the past comes back to haunt you.

The best thing my adoptive parents did was to enroll my sisters and me into a Catholic School. I fell in love with the prayers and traditions of the Catholic faith. In that first year, I was baptized, completed my First Confession, my First Communion, and I even played Mary in the Christmas play! I got involved in sports and music. I slowly stopped crying myself to sleep at night as I learned that God absolutely adores His children. Here was a Father who would not hurt and was there for me all the time.

Where I began to thrive, my older sister began to exhibit mental illness symptoms similar to our biological mother's until it came to complete fruition. She was a senior in high school, pregnant, suicidal and at a breaking point. She disclosed to a counselor that she had been sexually abused by our foster brother.

At first I was furious. Why are you telling our business? Why can't you just let it go? It's supposed to be our secret!

Then, I knew I had to help her in order for her to heal because our adoptive parents did not believe her. I confirmed her truth despite still trying to hide mine. In the end we were told by the investigators that too many years had passed, that the investigation showed he had violated other children, but essentially nothing was going to be done.

Through the years I have spoken with therapists and have done the work to deal with the pain and anger I had about this person that snatched my innocence. I learned my brokenness is not a determent to God's Purpose. Through the totality of my experiences and the work I have done, it has given me the ability to unlock doors in my profession of being a police officer. I am able to share wisdom and insight with domestic violence and sexual assault victims. My Super Power is getting victims to see that they don't deserve to be hurt and leading them to the help that is available. I believe I am fulfilling my purpose and living the life that I was created to do. So many times while I am speaking with a victim, I say a silent prayer, "Dear God, use me to speak to this person. Speak through me with the words that will get them to the space where they will accept help and do better for themselves and their family."

It is in those times when I feel the same Holy Spirit moving through me, the same energy that was with me that night when I was kneeling in the snow as a seven-year-old girl looking up at the star filled night sky knowing in my heart that we are loved by God, and everything will be okay. Recalling that winter night in 1983 where I had the strength to guide my mother and lead us to my teacher's house to safety, I am reminded of my favorite poem by Max Ehrmann, "You are a child of the universe, no less than the trees and the stars; you have a right to be here. And whether or not it is clear to you, no doubt the universe is unfolding as it should."

"God began to answer my prayers with the Hope In God group.
These women have let me cry on their shoulders.
They have prayed for me and encouraged me."

BJYounger, OSB
2017

"Rejoice in hope, be patient in tribulation, be constant in prayer. Bless those who persecute you; bless and do not curse them. Rejoice with those who rejoice, weep with those who weep."

Romans 12:12,15

Diane's Story

I was raised in small town South Dakota. I always believed and trusted Jesus! I had three sisters, two brothers, and one younger brother who passed away as an infant. We moved from one small town to a little bigger town.

My mom and dad ended up getting a divorce after 24 years of being married. This was difficult on all of us children. I questioned what it was I did wrong to cause it to happen. I loved both of my parents and wanted them to be together. When all was said and done, they ended up   remarrying and basically doing a spouse swap. My dad only lived half a block away, so if he did have time for us, which was not very often, we did not have far to go. My step dad was an amazing man. After I grew up enough to know, coming into a house of mouthy, bratty, teenage, sad and depressed kids was no easy task to take on.   He did it with such grace and mercy - something I was unaware existed. God bless him.

My two older sisters, Mary and Kate started dating. Within what seemed to be no time at all, they were planning to have a double wedding. That didn't work out, but they married less than a month apart. We have always been a very close family. Many of us did things together and only had a few close friends outside of our own tight knit family. Six months after my sister Mary married her husband Adam, who was attending mechanic training in Minneapolis, Mary decided to go with. She became very ill while there. Unsure of what was causing Mary to be so ill, Adam called his parents to help find a way to get her back to their hometown doctor. My two sets of parents and Adam's parents all went to be with her. She was 21 years old and in a very fragile state.

My other older sister Kate was taking care of us while our parents were with Mary in hopes of figuring out what was making her so ill. Kate still made us go to school. Many times growing up, even in circumstances such as this, things that are going on, such as the unknown of whether our sister was going to get better or not, was typically ignored and not discussed, but then we were to go on like there was nothing wrong. My family was great at sweeping troubles under the rug and forgetting about them, hoping they did not surface again.

The first day of class the teacher asked how things were, and I broke down crying in front of everyone. It was so embarrassing. I was sent to the nurse's office. Eventually, all of us children were sent home. Mary lived three days. She passed away surrounded by her husband and all of the parents, all who loved her very much. It was discovered later in an autopsy she had bacteria in her blood, now known as leukemia. We got through the funeral, and in the coming months afterward, it was difficult for us to process. Adam lived with us for about year after her death just to work on getting back up on his feet. Things seemed to be back to normal.

One day, Jeff, Kate's husband, came to our house and said I was supposed to go to his and my sister's house because she needed talk to me. I was barely ten or eleven. Much of my life, it felt as though she disliked me no matter what I did to try to please her. I was always trying to come up with ideas how to make her love me more. When we got to their house, she was not there. I knew in my heart something was not right. Panic set in. I felt something horribly wrong. Jeff then told me my sister wanted him to teach me right from wrong, and it did not involve a game, spankings, or anything I had endured in the past. This was something new to try. I tried to run out the door, but he stopped me. My throat fell to the pit of my stomach. I felt awful, dirty, guilty, and unworthy. He proceeded to force me to grope him, and he put his filthy hands all over my body. When his evil desires still had not been met, he forced me to perform oral sex on him. He began to try to stimulate me orally. With each touch and movement, I felt my self-worth slip further and further away from me. He took all my clothes off of me, and forced himself inside of my vagina. It felt as though it was being ripped apart. It hurt so badly. I wanted to scream and yell, but he made sure I couldn't.

This happened several more times. After each time, he was sure to tell me that if I told anyone, no one would believe me, and I would be the one at fault, and he would be sure I paid for it. I finally had the confidence to confide in a Spanish girlfriend of mine, and we talked with her dad. He wanted me to go to the police, but I told him I would first like to talk to my mom and sister. I didn't talk to them right away. The fear of being blamed and no one believing me took over. When I finally got the courage up to disclose what was going on, I was blamed for being too promiscuous. I was told to just get over it, and no one would be going to the authorities. It felt as though my mouth had been sewn shut. The abuse continued to happen until my sister moved to Rapid City. I then thought I was finally free. No more abuse...Wrong! Jeff and Kate came home for a National Guard weekend, and he acted as if there was nothing wrong in his doings. He was King, and people bowed down to him. He could do no wrong. His abusive attacks became more forceful and vicious. Jeff's abuse occurred on a regular basis when they would visit. I always did my best to hide it and pretend like nothing happened, but it got more and more difficult to pretend and put a smile on my face

Eventually, I married and had my son. We were at my mom's house visiting. Jeff was in town, so when he stopped over for a visit, he gave me the look he always had right before he forced himself on me. I was so afraid, so I quickly went home and locked my door. My son and I hid in the bedroom. Furious, Jeff followed us to my house. I could hear every step he took as he approached my front door. He was furious with me for running away. I remember thinking it felt as though a giant was searching for me, and it was just a matter of time before I was found. I didn't answer the door, and finally, after several angry pounds on the door and windows, he left. I released a huge sigh of relief.

I knew it was time, so I finally confided in my husband about the abuse. He was so angry with Jeff. We finally sat my mom, Kate and Jeff down, and discussed the abuse. Even though they heard what had happened, it still felt as though it was my fault. I was the one to blame, a common feeling I carried throughout my childhood, if you can all it that. Finally, the abuse stopped.

I remember questioning, "What did I do, God? I tried to be good!" I never really felt as though he answered my prayers. I decided if God didn't care, well nobody would. I pushed Him further and further away throughout my life. I plunged myself neck deep into drugs, alcohol, and whatever I could do to numb the feelings and forget about what a horrible person I felt like I was. God was doing small things in my life, but I never gave Him the credit. I would chalk it up to karma, or coincidence.

Finally a year ago, God began to answer my prayers with the Hope In God group. These women have let me cry on their shoulders. They have prayed for me and encouraged me. This time, my eyes are wide open, waiting to see what God has in store for my life and my story. Slowly, my faith in Him is being restored.

"I finally let go and gave it to God.
I took the lid off of the pot and let God make a wonderful creation!"

BJYounger, OSB
2017

"And Jesus awoke and rebuked the wind and said to the sea, Peace! Be still! And the wind ceased, and there was a great calm."

Mark 4:39 (ESV)

Claire's Story

I always discounted my story. I thought I had no right to be mad or angry; there were many others who suffered worse than I. I have come to realize that what happened to me did matter. I did not have to hold all that pain inside; I did my best at trying though. Every time I share my story I free myself from that pain and take my life back. I would like this to be just one incident, one nightmare to get over. However, there have been three times in my life where my strength, my sense of self was threatened. I liken my life to that of a pot of boiling water. The pain was always there bubbling away, ready to burn me. The more I left the lid on the pot of water the more it bubbled over.

I was twenty when my sister talked to me about what happened to me when I was about five. I could not remember, and I was extremely angry at her for saying that something did happen. Denial and confusion set in. That conversation opened the memories that had been stored in my mind. My mind flew back to that day; memories like waves came crashing down on me. I remember the smell of sweat and dirt. The neighbor boy who I thought was my friend wanted to show me this spot. We were in a tent-like structure, magazines with naked women strung all over the floor. Fear came bubbling up like a pot of boiling water. I wanted to put a lid on this boiling pot of fear, shame and anger.

I had repressed these memories, held that lid on the pot for over a decade. The more I tried to keep the lid on the pot, the more burns I got. These burns came forth in self harm, eating disorders, anger, fighting, and drinking. All of these helped me hold down that lid, but they all left scars, and unfortunately, I could not keep that lid on. Those negative behaviors only helped add pressure under the lid. How could that have happened to me? Why did I not remember that? Why when I called my mother at the age of 20 to tell her about what happened to me she told me, "Oh well. That was your father's fault"? Why did she never acknowledge my pain or try to sooth the hurt? It was then that I chose to tuck this memory away again. That did not work so well. Like a pot of boiling water, the memories, shame and confusion came bubbling over into my life again.

Years later I was on vacation with my family. I was only eleven. I had the time of my life in beautiful Mexico. We made some great memories. I remember how the native culture was in awe of my white blonde hair. The warm salty air, the soft sand, beautiful green, blue ocean, the different foods and the music. Then came the day to leave; we had befriended some people who worked at the resort we had been staying at, and it was time to say goodbye. I remember our goodbyes, a man I stupidly trusted. When he came to say goodbye, he went to give me what I thought was going to be a hug. Instead, he put his hand in the spot I had always been told was the private spot, the family jewels. He went to kiss me sticking his disgusting tongue in my mouth. Fear and shame came rushing back into me. I held down that lid of boiling water even tighter.

I was fifteen, fearless and thought I was tough. I had a reputation as a badass. I had been in more fights than most guys my age.

That night I found out how wrong I was. That night my friends and I went to a party, and I tried pot for the first time. My friends left the party without me. Another friend got his friend to give me a ride home. It was past my curfew, and I knew I would be in trouble if I couldn't sneak into the house. I thought I would be safe. He was my friend's friend, and I was tough... I was wrong again.

Immense, crippling, paralyzing fear came over me as his arm became a vice around my neck. Scratching, pulling and fighting, I couldn't get loose from his strong hold around my neck. Bright light, gasping for air, confusion. I felt separated and numb from my body as he then forced me to do disgusting things. I don't know how, and I don't know why, but I got away and I ran. I ran home where there was a police car parked in front of my house. Fear and shame again... I snuck in the basement window and went to the bathroom. I remember scrubbing myself with the hottest water I could to get that horrible evil off of me. I did finally go upstairs and faced my mother and the police officer. My mother had called the police when I was late coming home. I was lectured on being late and going to a party. I kept up the act for awhile until I finally released what had just happened to me. I wouldn't tell them the guy's name. I was too ashamed. I couldn't let anyone know and find out how horrible and disgusting I was. I could cover up the bruises on my outer skin, but my self esteem took an even further blow. I tried even harder to hold down that lid.

For many years I believed there had to be something bad about me, that I had been doing something wrong. Why else would this have happened to me again and again? For years I punished myself. I was obsessive about my weight. I took stupid chances. I even tried to take my own life. Nothing would ease that pain. I was lucky though. I fell in love with the most amazing, kind, patient man. I let God in. Before, I would get angry with God for letting this happen to me. Once I was able to let God in, I realized he did not "let" this happen to me, but he did give me the strength and courage to make it through this and come out stronger.

I had many chances in my life to let someone help me. I wish I would have let someone in. I could have started the healing process so much sooner. I was a bunch of could have and should haves. I finally chose to heal. I let people help me. I realized that God helped me get through this, and from this I could help others. What happened to me will always be a part of my life. It did change me. I chose to make this a change for the better. I finally let it go and gave it to God. I took the lid off of the pot and let God make a wonderful creation!

"God didn't leave you. God protected your heart...A huge eagle flew under me and transported me to the other side."

BJyounger, OSB
2017

"...for he has said, I will never leave you nor forsake you. So we can confidently say,
The Lord is my helper;
   I will not fear;
what can anyone do to me?"
Hebrews:13:5b-6

Mary's Story

"It was the best of times, it was the worst of times." *A Tale of Two Cities* by Charles Dickens opens with this quote, and the book expresses the hope of resurrection and transformation in a hopeless situation. That's the tale of my life as well.

I came from a large family with abusive parents in a community that didn't talk about what happened behind closed doors. The summer before I started kindergarten, a relative invited me along with him to deliver gas to several farms around our home town. I adored this relative who often showed me favor over my other siblings. I took a bath, and found my prettiest dress. I fixed my hair and waited impatiently on the front step for him to drive up. He finally arrived, smiling big as he picked me up and swung me around before lifting me into the big truck. I felt special and happy. I remember thinking, "This is the best day of my life!"

I played with the farmers' children, chased chickens, ate cookies, and laughed with this man that I loved and trusted. My best day came to a screeching halt and reversed into the worst day when this man brutally raped me on the way home. I reported that abuse right away to another relative. She called me a liar and a whore, beat me, and screamed, "Shut up!" I shut up more than my voice. I buried those memories deep in the dark basement of my soul, locked them tight, and covered them with fear, shame, and self-hatred.

I spent the rest of my childhood trying to earn my parents' love by taking care of my little brothers and sisters, doing laundry, grocery shopping, washing dishes, and making meals. I earned straight A's in school and tried to succeed at everything in order to prove my worth. In high school I switched to trying to please my friends and began to drink and party. I always felt ugly, dirty, and worthless. I continued on this path into college. Hope began in my life when I met my husband the end of my freshman year. He saw what I never could see. He saw who God created me to be.

I married him my junior year, and we grew close as I disclosed the pain of emotional and physical abuse, but still did not have any concrete memories of being sexually abused. When I found out I was pregnant 3 years later, I panicked. I had read the statistics in my Psychology class - children who were abused are more likely to abuse their own children. I was so frightened, but soon embraced the joy of life when I felt my child move for the first time.

The day I gave birth to my daughter also fell into that category of best day and worst day. Our nurse panicked when the baby decided to come faster than normal. She actually asked my husband if he was sure this was my first baby. She screamed at me not to push when it was clearly time to push. As I tried not to push and the pain was ripping through my body, the barricaded memories of being sexually abused came tumbling out. When they put my little girl on my chest, I carefully touched her thick dark hair. She screamed, and my soul screamed louder as disjointed pictures of a sad little girl crying alone in her bed came flooding in. I rocked my baby, but she screamed louder and wouldn't stop crying until her daddy said, "Hello there, Baby." She suddenly stopped and looked at him with her piercing blue eyes.

When the nurse took her and cleaned her up and took her temperature, she announced that our little girl was too cold and needed the incubator. I panicked and urged my husband, "Go with her. Don't leave her alone!" And then I was all alone with my memories as the doctor stitched me up. My legs started to shake uncontrollably.

"Are you cold?" he asked.

"Yes!" He brought me blankets and started again.

"Ouch!"

He stopped. "Didn't you have an epidural?"

"No. I felt every single thing."

"Well, we sure don't see that much. I'll get you something for the pain." As he stuck the needle in, I wondered to myself if the piercing shame wracking my heart would ever stop. As the physical pain subsided and the emotional pain rose, I tried to push it down like before. It refused to stay down. Sleep eluded me that night, while my whole body shook under the heavy weight of blankets that couldn't warm me.

When we brought our baby home, I loved every moment of feeding her and caring for her until she started to cry. Every time she cried, a new memory surfaced. My heart beat fast, sweat ran down my face, and the urge to run would tempt me. One day I almost dropped my sweet child during a particularly violent memory. I put her down in the bassinet and ran downstairs. I pulled a load of clothes out of the washer and kneeled down to put them into the dryer. Grief rose up, tears fell down my face, and a wail came up from the deep. "God, you have to help me! I can't do this any more. I'm afraid I'll hurt my baby if this doesn't end. Please! I can't do this. I need help! Please help me!"

And the doorbell rang. I dried my tears, ran up the stairs, and found our pastor at the door. "Hello there! I just came by to bring these cookies my wife made and to congratulate you on the new baby!" He was all smiles as I invited him in and took the cookies.

"I was just downstairs praying for help, and God answered by sending you to my door at the very minute I asked. I guess He really is real."

The smile disappeared, our pastor looked absolutely terrified, and asked if he could pray for me. I agreed and he prayed at lightning speed for me and the baby. Then he made excuses about his busy day and left. I stood at the door and waved goodbye with shame coloring my face. I tried praying for myself and just sat there until I had an idea. The pastor was no help, but I remembered that the local college offered free counseling. I forgot all about it that afternoon until the baby started to cry again and this time would not stop.

When my husband came home that evening, I handed him the wailing baby and yelled, "I'm going for a walk. I need to get out of here." He looked frightened but said okay as I ran out the door. I ran, yes, physically ran all the way to the college campus ministry office and told the receptionist I didn't have an appointment but I needed to talk to someone. The counselor just happened to be there doing some paperwork with her newborn baby sleeping in a car seat next to her desk. She listened intently to my story.

"Am I going crazy? Am I going to hurt my baby?"

"Do you want to hurt your baby?"

"No way!"

"You were seriously abused. You have been in denial all these years. It's kind of like shock when you have been in a traumatic accident. It keeps you alive until you can get help. You need time to process all the anger and grieve what you've lost. Crazy people and child abusers don't ask for help. You asked for help, and I'm here to help. You don't have to do this alone. You're going to be okay."

Over the next year, piece by piece of sounds, smells, flashes of body parts, and crazy bits and pieces of my life were uncovered and remembered and my whole disjointed life began to finally make sense. These days were excruciatingly painful and full of hope all at once. I learned how to love my daughter, my husband, and then myself.

When I moved to another town and my daughter turned 5, fear returned and I found another counselor. After a few sessions, she asked me to tell her what I remembered about being sexually abused. As I told my story, she began to cry. Her tears puzzled and shocked me.

"Where were you when these things were happening to you? When you tell your story, you tell it as an observer. As though you weren't there."

"I wasn't there. I went far away into the sky into a blue warm cloud-like thing."

She asked me to paint it and bring it with me to the next meeting. She looked at it and cried again. "This isn't a cloud or a womb. Look. These are hands. God's hands. He was holding you together. God was holding you and crying and keeping your fragile soul from flying apart into a million pieces. God didn't leave you. God protected your heart."

And then it was my turn to cry for a lost childhood and stolen innocence. I did the hard work of forgiving my abusers and everyone who knew and didn't report. I stopped trying to hide the shame of what happened to me. I chose to accept the reality of how it hurt me.

Before that day in the counselor's office, I had a recurring dream. I would be running in the dark with a hideous monster chasing me. I could feel and smell his filthy breath on the back of my neck. I screamed and ran through the dark until I reached the edge of a high cliff. I would always wake up just as the monster got close enough to reach out his claws and almost grab me. That night I had the same dream, but as the monster reached out his claws to seize me, I jumped off the cliff. Free falling through the air didn't frighten me! I put my arms and legs out and enjoyed the ride. Suddenly, a huge eagle flew under me and transported me to the other side. Those old nightmares never returned.

"It was the best of times, it was the worst of times, it was the age of wisdom, it was the age of foolishness, it was the epoch of belief, it was the epoch of incredulity, it was the season of Light, it was the season of Darkness, it was the spring of hope, it was the winter of despair, we had everything before us..." A Tale of Two Cities by Charles Dickens

"God is the ultimate healer....He can break all chains that have been holding you down. You just have to lift your head up, look past your own wounds, stop swimming in your own misery, pain and tribulation, and look up."

"Now the Lord is the Spirit, and where the Spirit of the Lord is, there is freedom."

2 Corinthians 3:17

Susan's Story

I walked into a counselor's office with feet that felt like big cement bricks. I didn't know what I needed. I just knew that my life felt like a broken mirror, and I could not put these shattered pieces together. It was a dark and completely hopeless feeling like I had been wandering through a desert and couldn't find a trusted shelter anywhere. I had moments when I felt as if I was being pulled down into a deep grave with dark clouds and negative thoughts that wouldn't stop whispering in my ear.

The receptionist told me what it would cost for a session of counseling according to my income, and I took a seat in the waiting room. I stared blankly into my checkbook, and tears welled up in my eyes. I knew I could not make this work since my husband didn't want me to be here in the first place. I felt weary like I could faint, but soon a panic rose up inside me like an angry dragon, and I felt I needed to escape. As I stood up and turned to leave, a woman softly appeared in the doorway and called my name. I told her I could not be here; he didn't want me here, and I couldn't afford this. She stepped to the side almost as if to guard me from running out. Her steady, calm voice asked me to just step back into her office and talk to her as she extended her arm gently to guide me. I took a chance, and I followed her lead.

I don't remember talking to her for a whole hour. I didn't know what was the matter with me, or why I was so unhappy. Now it seems like a brief moment in time. She asked questions, and I answered with tissues wadded up in my fists. I didn't look up much, and my fingers kept tracing the hole in my jeans. I had been to a counselor before when my brother committed suicide, but he never delved too deep into my past. Melanie had soft, brown hair and eyes that were inviting but not intrusive. She seemed so calm and patient with me. The angry storms that gathered over my home constantly seemed distant if just for a moment. My past relationships were also tumultuous, and a pattern was emerging going back through my history. Then Melanie hit the nail on the head and caught me completely off guard, "Susan, were you ever sexually abused as a child?" No one had ever asked me this before let alone talk about it. "Yes," I stammered. "I was. I was molested by three different men when I was seven years old." Did she really just ask me that?

The hour seemed to come to an end just as this closet door had been opened. Melanie asked me to come back and talk to her again, and I told her I could not. I explained my husband did not want me there, and I could not afford this. Melanie explained I would be put on a grant for abused women. "You think I am abused?" She nodded gently. "You mean I wouldn't have to pay for another session?" She said it would be taken care of, and I should not worry about anything but coming back to see her. Well, I didn't have that excuse to not come back, but I told her I wanted to get counseling with my husband, but he refused to come in with me. Melanie stated that she would just start with counseling me, and maybe later we could see what happened.

When I walked outside with an appointment card in my hand finding the hour had flown by, a rainstorm had kissed the town in the meantime. The dark clouds in the distance were rolling away, and the sun was starting to peak through. Everything smelled so clean, and the busy traffic continued to rush by on Highway 212. As I stared at a puddle that reflected the sunset, a car disturbed the reflection and splashed the puddle to the side. I felt a small awakening of hope inside.

I went to Lutheran Social Services for nearly two years. I won't try to fool you; this was a very painful time in my life. Looking into a mirror at our behaviors takes strength to touch our wounds. I read books, studied abuse and learned how it damages the soul. I had been through several abusive relationships and couldn't seem to break the cycle, but I had a breakthrough during a session one day in my mid-thirties. I discovered that I blamed that little seven year old girl for what happened that first day. When the policeman came to my home to take the report, I seriously thought I was going to jail that night. My parents never talked to me about the abuse. No one talked to me about sex or what happened. It was just swept under the rug as it seemed to be back in the 60's. I had been having flashbacks of his rotten teeth in my face while he touched me. I realized in therapy that every time this happened to me, that someone was using me for their pleasure without thinking once how this could damage a little girl. And I also realized that I blamed myself for the bad things that happened, and I associated the pleasures that God had intended for marriage had been disturbed and twisted into sin in my mind instead. Studying my past showed how I continued my low self-esteem throughout my childhood. I carried this baggage unknowingly into my adulthood. I had no clue I was doing this to myself until my breakthrough opened this Pandora's Box.

And just when I seemed to be stuck in this pain of what happened to me as a child, I heard my pastor in church one Sunday morning talk about our tribulations. Our struggles and hurts we go through can serve a greater purpose if we take those wounds and turn them around to help others. In the eye of my storm, I felt a light go on over my head. I felt this was my purpose, and I needed to help others deal with the effects of child sexual abuse. But I had my work cut out for me.

You see, when I was growing up I did not go to church. I never read the Bible. I had friends going to church but didn't think too much of it. I had relatives who were attending a very legalistic church, and it seemed that they had a peg on going to heaven. They condemned going to movies, playing cards, the music I liked, and of course divorce was leading a person to hell. My parents had divorced, and we moved to Norfolk, NE, so I spent more time with these family members. Eventually, I felt there was no hope for me going to heaven, so why even try? I now realize I was carrying this hidden baggage with me anyway. I became promiscuous as a teen. I never thought I had something precious to save for someone. Looking back, I see my self-esteem was very low which in the end led me into bad relationships.

My first marriage ended with hiding his shotgun in one closet and the shells in another closet in another room. He had held his gun to my temple for over an hour one night pushing me around with the gun before shooting the 30 gallon octagon aquarium in the end. The smell of gunpowder hung heavy in the air. The shag carpet was soaked with water, glass and fish flopping around gasping for air. My memories of it are in slow motion. That could have been my brains. I escaped after one year only to quickly enter another relationship that was unhealthy. I did not love myself enough to expect anything better for myself. I also had been held down and my face burned with a cigarette in one case. I never wanted to get divorced, ever, but it reaffirmed that I was a bad person and was only going to hell. I thought I could handle the bruises and name calling, but words can cut like a knife. They can be vicious and evil. I was conditioned to believe the horrible things said to me not to mention what this did to my children.

In order to try anything to save my marriage, I went to church one Easter. I remember crying uncontrollably in church that day when they described the crucifixion. They told how Jesus was pierced in the side to make sure he was dead. Isaiah 53:5, "But he was pierced for our rebellion, crushed for our sins. He was beaten so we could be whole. He was whipped so we could be healed." I couldn't believe Jesus would love me enough to die for me. The word "heal" is used in some form 138 times in the Bible, as Jesus is the ultimate Healer. He wanted to help me, but I cried because it was too hard to believe. How could he love me?

At the end of my marriage, I found myself bawling into my pillow. I cried so hard my stomach ached, and I drenched my pillow with tears and makeup. I cried out to God over and over for what seemed like hours. I cried out asking him what love is anyway. I kept repeating I didn't know what love was and asked him what is was. I fell into a deep sleep with no tears left to expel. The next morning while getting ready for work, I was in the shower. I heard "Corinthians 13." This was not an audible voice but more like a thought. While putting makeup on my swelled up eyes, I heard "Corinthians 13." During my drive to work I heard "Corinthians 13." I had never read the Bible. At that time I hadn't gone to church much my whole life, so it really didn't mean much to me, except I knew it was from the Bible. When I got to work, I began my daily rituals of getting my inks out and beginning my job as a touch-up-artist. While painting, I heard this same message. My boss approached me with a warm greeting. He knew I was going through a tough time for years now, and it had recently boiled to a head with ending in a protection order against my husband. I turned to him deep in thought and asked him a question instead of greeting him back. "You have read the Bible. You go to church, so can you tell me something please? What is Corinthians 13?" His eyes searched for an answer, but he couldn't recall at that moment. We both shrugged our shoulders, and with that he went to his office. It was only a few minutes later when he came back to me with papers in his hand. When I took the papers, I saw the title. I nearly dropped the cup of ink I was holding. At the top of the page it said, "What is Love? Corinthians 13." As I began to read the verse I had heard before, God described what love is supposed to be. But the words on the page seemed bold and jumped out at me telling me what love is NOT supposed to be. Everything He said love was supposed to be was not what I had in my marriage. Everything He said love was NOT was what I had in my marriage. My eyes opened as wide as saucers, not because I learned what love should be like, but because the God of the Universe spoke to me! He heard my cries. He heard my question, and he specifically answered it. I about fell off my work platform.

He heard me. He hears you too. Psalm 34:18, "The Lord is close to the brokenhearted; he rescues those whose spirits are crushed."

I had never learned about Grace. Amazing grace is what God offers us free of charge! He loves us unconditionally, and we only have to accept it. He did not want me to go to hell. Instead, He was extending His hand to me all those years, but I had my head down and was hiding from Him. I never thought I was worthy of His love. I wanted to keep leading my life the way I wanted and did not want to give up anything to follow Him. I thought He was going to take away the things I THOUGHT made me happy. Once I realized that He loved me and accepted me right where I was at, I started to turn around and listen to Pastor Spahr's sermons. My oldest daughter talked me into trying a church when she was a teen. It changed my life. All the books I read about abuse and self-help were good material, but nothing seemed to equal the living waters that come rushing through you when you fully dive in. I had gone to church at Easter and Christmas for years but realized I was only dipping my toes in the water. The more I sought Him, the more I found Him. I didn't have to climb any ladders of deeds; I just had to accept His Grace. I took the plunge and was baptized. I am new, I am reborn, and this has brought me more profound happiness than I ever thought was possible. God is the ultimate Healer. He is the great Physician. He can break all the chains that have been holding you down. You just have to lift your head up, look past your own wounds, stop swimming in your own misery, pains and tribulation, and look up.

In an effort to search for a way of using my pain to help others, I started volunteering for everything. Sometimes we get so involved in so many things trying to make our own purpose happen. I became a mentor for Kids Hope USA. I joined the choir. I helped with youth group and setting up the altar for holidays with decorations and skits. I took every class I could take to learn more about God. I felt if I am going to lead others to Christ, then I need to know what I am talking about if they ask a question. I read the Bible and did book studies. I became a Congregational Care Minister and a Prayer Counselor. I took a class studying a book called *Hearing God's Voice*. This proved more helpful in understanding that I could not make my own purpose, but I had to pull back and ask God what He wanted me to do, what His purpose was for me. The doors open up when we listen.

I saw a post on Facebook from my friend Jo about child sexual abuse, and I commented that this needs to be talked about more and not be hushed up, and this was the point leading up to becoming a working member for the Hope In God (H.I.G.) group she was forming. Prayer and meditation led to forming a group of ladies who can join in their struggles with childhood sexual abuse. I am now a co-leader with studying the book *Wounded Heart* by Dr. Dan B. Allender. A group of ladies have been learning about many traits that an adult survivor can carry with them such as ambivalence, shame, guilt , betrayal and powerlessness to name a few. We are learning to hand God our baggage, and he will help break the chains that have been holding us back, but the author leads the reader to know that God's grace wins every time. I no longer feel like a broken mirror. The Great I Am said I am beautiful. I am a masterpiece and a perfectly made work of art. And so I am.

"Allowing God to be our Lord is a process...
It is a journey...our significance comes from who we are in God
and who we are as part of humanity."

"Indeed, I count everything as loss because of the surpassing worth of knowing Christ Jesus my Lord. For his sake I have suffered the loss of all things and count them as rubbish, in order that I may gain Christ and be found in him, not having a righteousness of my own that comes from the law, but that which comes through faith in Christ, the righteousness from God that depends on faith."
Philippians 3:8-9 (ESV)

Chris' Story

On May 5, 2017, I am driving back home from a family gathering and feeling like the world is closing in on me. I am feeling empty and alone. I don't like that feeling anymore. Family has always been a challenge. I drive into the farm yard of my ex-husband's daughter. Not sure what to expect. It has been years since I had been here. A lot has changed, a new house and fenced in pastures. The tree groves are much bigger. I wonder if she was ever abused. She is not home. I am not sure what I would have done if she was.

I am still feeling panic, and my mind is racing. I start the car and drive back down the drive way and stop. I have the need to talk to someone. I need help. I texted a friend. She is at work, so I don't expect a response right away, but maybe this evening we can connect. I put the car in drive and turn on the road to head back to the main highway. It wasn't even fifteen minutes and she texted, "I am at work...Will call you in a little bit." The phone rang, and we talked for about a half hour as I was driving down the road. She has been helping me deal with my past for almost a year now as I just can't seem to let memories of sexual assaults, violence, and abuse in my marriage go. She has been very patient and listens when I talk. We end the conversation. I would be joining her at an event the next night.

It is now four days after the event. What an experience! The food, worship music, the lighting of the Chinese lanterns, and the bonfire included a time of sharing and prayers. The message is what got my attention the most. My friend along with a pastor shared the Road to Emmaus – Luke 24:13-35, "Now that same day two of them was going to a village called Emmaus about seven miles from Jerusalem. ... They asked each other, "Were not our hearts burning within us while he talked with us on the road and opened the Scriptures to us? ...." and the 23rd Psalm – "The Lord is my shepherd; I shall not want. He makes me lie down in green pastures. He leads me beside still waters. He restores my soul. He leads me in paths of righteousness for his name's sake. Even though I walk through the valley of the shadow of death, I will fear no evil, for you are with me; your rod and your staff, they comfort me. You prepare a table before me in the presence of my enemies; you anoint my head with oil; my cup overflows"....I need to trust and let go. God is with me on this journey....So here is my story.

The first time I remember is when we three kids were at the bowling alley. The man used money and candy to get us to do what he wanted. Finally, we told our parents. My dad said the man had too much to drink and took him home. Another time I remember I was lying on the ground at the farm...my shirt was open and my pants were down to my knees...two older cousins were playing house. As a child, I observed and performed sexual activities that a child should never see or do. . .

I grew up on the family farm. My mother, father, brother, sister and I lived across from the garden in the big stone house where my aunt, uncle, and three cousins lived. My family worked hard on the farm. My uncle's family never had to do any of the chores on the farm. It was like my family was slaves to my uncle's family. By age 9, I was responsible for three to four hours of chores every night after school which consisted of milking cows by hand.

On Sundays, my aunt would need a ride into town to teach Sunday school, so my mother would drive her and all of us kids. My mother always stated that she was an atheist. My mother and father hardly ever attended church. The exception was the month of September when my dad was scheduled to usher.

I remember reading the Bible when I was young, so much that I broke the cover of the Bible. I asked my mom if I could have a new Bible. She asked the pastor for me. The pastor gave me a brand new one. We were poor with no running water in a three room house with five people living in it. I was always clothed in rummage sale clothing and hand me downs, getting something new was a luxury for me. I never really talked much as a child. My siblings, cousins, classmates, even the bus driver bullying me because of my weight. I believed all the things that were said were true at the time.

When I was a sophomore in high school, I was confirmed into the Lutheran faith. I attended Jr. and Sr. League. I wanted to learn more about Jesus and study the Bible. I soon got frustrated and quit going to Sr. League because we never opened the Bible. At that time, I was not getting along with my parents very well either. My two cousins (male and female) were my very best friends started a relationship between themselves. I was no longer part of the friendship.

As a senior in high school, I started hanging around the local bar. The summer after my senior year I house sat for an aunt and uncle while they were working down south for a couple of months. I had a job in town during the day and would hang out at the bar at night. One night I woke up with a start. My uncle who had been down south was in bed with me. He called my name. He had been drinking.

Fall approached, I needed to do something. My dad's dream was for my brother to live on the family farm. The army recruiter had suggested electronics, so I enrolled in an electronics course at the vocational school closest to home. To start with I stayed with a cousin who lived there. School was easy, never having to do any work outside of class. One night I was sleeping in our two bedroom apartment. We hardly ever saw each other. She worked second shift, I left the front door open. Awakened I heard my name being called – my cousin who had been also my friend was standing in the doorway to my bedroom. I could not fight him.

By now I was drinking a lot. I was working as a waitress on Thursday nights and a bartender at the bar back home on weekends. Most nights I would drink right along with the customers and smoke a couple packs of cigarettes.

The summer after my first year of vocational school I worked at a state park and bartended. On the third of July, my sister shot herself and was in the hospital. The conversation was she claimed she was raped. We never talked about it.

In the fall for my second year at the vocational school, I received a letter from my mother that she had left my dad. My dad and I are close, and I know it was not what my dad wanted. My mother left because she was tired of living with no running water and other stuff. I needed someone to talk to. I had a work study job. My instructor would come in and set up demonstrations for the next day's classes while I was there. He listened to me and had a genuine concern for me. One evening while I was working at the school, he made a pass at me. It surprised me, and I moved away and went home. Then one night he showed up at my apartment. I never told him where I lived. He had brought a bottle of liquor. Things got out of hand. What was done was done. He would show up every so often after that.

I never attended any church. It never even crossed my mind. The only time I would go to church is for a wedding or a funeral. I continued my college education. I had a part time job to make ends meet. I continued the life of drinking, smoking, partying and the sexual involvement during my college career. In December of 1987, I graduated with a Bachelor's of Science in Electrical Engineering.

The next spring, I was asked to consider teaching at the vocational school I had graduated from and started in July of 1988. I thought I should go to church since I was an instructor. Some of my co-workers attended a Lutheran church, so I would go now and again.

It was a Tuesday before Thanksgiving 1989. I was teaching my morning class. One of my co-workers came and got me and told me to come to the office and have a chair. All the staff was there. What was going on? "Your father was in a farm accident and was killed." My world fell apart, my dad was only 48 years old.

The family was still on the dairy farm. My mother ended up purchasing the farm from my uncle and aunt. My sister and her boyfriend moved home as hired hands. Help from me was not wanted. I was alone, and I felt I no longer had a home to go to. So it was time to purchase my own home. Little did I know that the couple I purchased the home from would be the couple that brought me back to church. The wife encouraged me to go to Bible study on Thursday evenings. She also became a great friend. She was the grandmother figure that I never really had. And she was a Christian.

It is now spring of 1995. My brother and I had moved our mother out to a cabin on the lake. She was getting a divorce after a five year marriage. I was still teaching. When I came out of the office to go to class down the hall, there stood my mother and her husband. "Why are you here?"

"Your brother is dead. He shot himself." The pastor of the church I attended, the lady I purchased the house from, and a woman that I served on church council with attended the funeral. I was so surprised. There was no way my pastor could attend all the funerals of the church members. Pastor was very concerned for me. He connected me to a couple that mentored me weekly for a couple of months to assist me with dealing with my brother's suicide. I was also asked to go on a mission trip to Fortaleza, Brazil, with a team. These experiences had a great impact on me. As a result, I became very active in the church and began attending church services and Bible studies regularly.

In 1998 a friend of mine and co-worker asked me to marry him. This was a dream come true. We both sold our houses and built a new home at the lake. We were married August 21, 1998. I will never forget it. I was shaking as we were taking our vows. I was making a promise before God and everyone in that church.

His oldest daughter did not show up for the wedding. My husband and I still worked together. The marriage very quickly became a struggle for me. Less than a month after we were married, his youngest daughter confronted us with regards to our having a relationship before marriage. After my husband and his youngest daughter took a walk around the block, he left and went hunting for the weekend. I told her the truth about the relationship. There were more than two hours of talking and lots of tears. Her older sister was in town too. She asked if I would share this with her sister. I said yes, but the oldest daughter would not come to the house. I knew now that the marriage was a mistake. My husband did not want to disclose to his children he had a relationship with me prior to our marriage.

To keep busy I went back to school and received my Master's degree the spring of 2003. This along with full-time teaching helped me get through each day. My friends and family would not come visit anymore. My husband made everyone feel unwelcome and never wanted me to spend any free time with anyone but him. My husband was very controlling and would go into rages. If things did not go his way, he would become mad. One night we were coming back from a hunting trip. It was around 1:00 a.m., and I had fallen asleep. I woke up and the pickup was shaking. I looked over at the speedometer and the needle was over 140 miles an hour. I asked him if he was trying to kill us both. About that time we hit a deer. It snapped him out of it, and he stopped the vehicle to take a look. No damage. THANK YOU GOD!! It was no fun doing anything with him any more…fishing, boating, hunting, dancing; even going out to dinner was a show.

It was now spring break of 2003. I am traveling to Pullman, Washington, to be with my college roommate. Her husband had passed away the week before. I was the first person to be with her. I helped her and her daughter plan her husband's funeral. He was only 48. I was one of their witnesses when they got married at the court house. One evening she and I were sitting at her dining room table and she asked me, "You are a Christian, aren't you? Why? I am empty inside and don't know what to do."

I told her that when you are part of a Christian community, you have support and help when you need it the most. Christians are people, who will not let you down, and you can count on them, and they love you.

I was not able to stay for the funeral. I returned home on Wednesday, so I could unpack and repack to do some training in Huron. My husband was not too happy about that. He wanted to know when I was going to spend time with him. He drove down to

Huron on Thursday and spent the night. That was the last time. I was done.

It is now Saturday morning, December 17, 2005. I'm alone, feeling sick to my stomach, and apprehensive. I should be feeling happy and grateful. It is the Christmas season. I am telling myself I should not be feeling this way. I am married, have a career, and am living at the lake in our dream home. The door opens. I am pulled out of my thoughts. My heart starts pounding and in he comes. He looks at me and asks, "What is for supper?" Are you kidding me, what is for supper? I had no idea when he was coming home.

The day before, I had been at a business meeting over the lunch hour. My husband and I had planned on going on an end of the season pheasant hunting trip for the weekend. By 2:00 p.m. that day I felt sick and called to tell my husband I did not feel well. He went without me. I got home shortly after 3:00 p.m. I was alone and had all evening for sure and part of tomorrow to think. I was struggling, I was thinking divorce. If I didn't get out of there, I was going to be lying beside my brother in the cemetery. SUICIDE? YES, SUICIDE. How could this be?

I had been praying for answers. God answered my prayers. He knew that I was in an abusive marriage. God provided friends, family, counseling, and the court system over the next year while obtaining a divorce.

I purchased a new home closer to where I worked. Ironically, the house address contained "316." It reminded me of John 3:16, "For God so loved the world that he gave his one and only Son, that whoever believes in him shall not perish but have eternal life". I was attending church regularly and serving on the stewardship committee. I was attending Bible studies and volunteering every free moment I had when I was not buried in my career. I was doing all the right things a Christian woman does, right? Then why was I still feeling angry, hopeless and empty inside?

Jump ahead a couple of years; I resigned from my teaching position of 20 years in the spring of 2008. I didn't know what my plans were going forward, but I needed to take a step back. It was more than six months before I secured a full time position. In the interim, fall came and I volunteered and substitute taught and continued to be active with Bible studies and church.

In December of 2008, a friend stopped me and asked if I had heard. Heard what? "You need to go visit him." Really? Visit my ex-husband? You have to be joking. I had made sure I kept my distance ever since the divorce. Several weeks passed, and again I was asked to go see him. With my trusted friend's advice I went for a visit. I was nervous not knowing for sure what I would be walking into. We visited for an hour. His health had deteriorated.

Several weeks had passed. In January 2009, on a Sunday morning after church while shopping, I met my ex-husband's youngest daughter. I had not seen her since the divorce. We visited, and the suggestion was made to go see him. He had fallen, broken his hip, and was in a care facility. I was assured it would work to go visit him that night. As I entered the room, he looked at me and asked me to pull up a chair beside the bed. We visited for a couple of hours. He was sorry for all the things he had done. He told me never stop being who I was. I left that evening feeling that God had answered my prayers. I needed to hear those words from him. I never understood how someone I loved at one time could hurt me so deeply. I returned to visit two more times that week. On Saturday as I stepped to go into the room, his two daughters were there. I was not welcome. The oldest daughter signaled me to go, so I turned and left.

He passed away that evening. A friend came and picked me up to attend his funeral. At the funeral the first lesson was from Ecclesiastes 3:2-15 verse 15, "That which is, already has been; that which is to be, already has been; and God seeks what has been driven away." Then Psalm 121, "My Help Comes From the Lord" and the second lesson 1 Corinthians 13:1-13 "The Way of Love," verses 4-6, "Love is patient and kind; love does not envy or boast; it is not arrogant or rude. It does not insist on its own way; it is not irritable or resentful; it does not rejoice at wrong doing, but rejoices with the truth."

Seven years later during the spring of 2016, I was on my fifth full time position. I had moved to another city and back to Watertown, bought and sold houses. I attended a presentation on sex trafficking in my local community. After hearing the presentation, it brought up old wounds that I thought I had dealt with. I found myself frustrated and feeling alone again. How could I get rid of these feelings? I needed to talk about this, but who was I going to share this with? I felt ashamed and guilty for all the things that I had done. I had kept most of this bottled up inside. I sat in that church pew almost every Sunday to hear God's words and was told over and over again by several pastors over the years to trust God. Jesus was my salvation and to put all of my troubles and worries on him. I was as white as snow and pure in heart. Why couldn't I believe that?

Finally God provided the answer. My friend Jo asked if I would consider being a board member for the Hope in God (H.I.G) group she was forming. Soon after that Jo asked if I would consider leading a mentoring ministry. *Heartwood* is available for women survivors of child sexual abuse, sexual assault, and domestic violence. *Heartwood* is an opportunity for women to walk together in relationship. All of us are traveling towards union with God and with every step we take, He is restoring us piece by piece.

Allowing God to be our Lord is a process which occurs over the course of our lifetimes. It is a journey which involves suffering, failure, humiliation, and pain. Our stories are never just about us. Instead, our significance comes from who we are in God and who we are as part of humankind. In order for you and me to be useful to God, we have to "suffer to heal, lose to gain, die to rise, give all away to keep it" (Barbara Younger).

The Apostle Paul said it like this, "For me to live in Christ, and to die is gain" (Philippians 1:21). In dying to self, we live in Christ. When we become void of ourselves, the Holy Spirit transforms us into the voice, hands and feet of Christ. In the Book of Ezekiel, God promises us, "And I will give you a new heart, and I will put a new spirit in you. I will take out your stony, stubborn heart and give you a tender, responsive heart." Ezekiel 26:36(NLT)

Much like the heartwood of a tree, the very core of our being must die and rot away. With God's grace, each of us has to surrender the center of our consent – the very supreme court of our souls – to and for His purpose. As Christians, we have to put Christ at the very center of all that we know and all that we are (William James). We are not the source, but instead we are the instrument through which the Holy Spirit works and flows. *Heartwood* is a Christian mentoring ministry. It's about women saying "yes" to the invitation to walk with and grow in Jesus because we have already been claimed, named, and destined for glory (Denis Meier). This is my journey until now - to God be the Glory! We are all on the road to Emmaus.

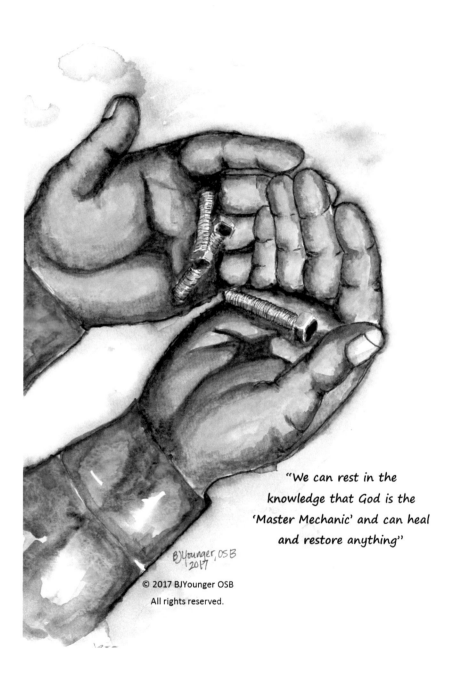

"We can rest in the
knowledge that God is the
'Master Mechanic' and can heal
and restore anything"

BJYounger, OSB
2017

"For by grace you have been saved through faith. And this is not your own doing; it is the gift of God, not a result of works, so that no one may boast. For we are his workmanship, created in Christ Jesus for good works, which God prepared beforehand, that we should walk in them."
Ephesians 2:8-10(ESV)

Jessica's Story

Imagine it's a beautiful spring day. The sun is shining bright, and there is a gentle breeze blowing through the barren trees. The spring buds have yet to break through to produce lush, green leaves. You're driving down the road soaking in the warmth of the sun through your windshield. The snow has all melted from the road ditches and fields. The fields are waiting for the new green life to break through the black top soil. This is the first day you have had absolutely nothing planned, no agenda, and no timeframe. This is a rarity in your life, and you take full advantage of your freedom. The next morning you wake like normal and start the day with the plans you have made. You get ready for work, let the dogs out and back in, pack your bag for the day and head out the door. When you start your vehicle, your tire monitoring system alerts you to a low tire. Not what you need. You had your plans laid out for the day, and this was not part of your agenda. Upon closer inspection you realize there is a bolt stuck in your tire. Air is slowly escaping causing your tire to go flat. Imagine your disappointment and frustration.

Proverbs 16:9 says, "In their hearts humans plan their course, but the Lord establishes their steps."

We as humans tend to plan our lives. We work hard to lay out all the details of our lives...when we come and go, where, and who we will connect with. We plan the big things such as jobs, college studies, marriages, family and the little things such as where we'll eat lunch, what time we will rise and what we will watch on TV. Sometimes we over compensate be becoming worriers, "Type A personalities," or "control freaks." This is especially true of anyone who has experienced events in their life where their power is robbed from them. No matter how hard we try to plan our lives and control different aspects of our lives, there are always going to be "bolts in the road" of life that are going to flatten our tires and change our plan.

One such bolt in my life was being molested by my father. I don't remember when it started, it was just always there. It became part of my "normal." This "normal" continued until I was 18 and moved to college. Even though I understood that this was not right and not the way a father/daughter relationship should be, I never disclosed this abuse to anyone until I got to college. The reason I never told was because I didn't want to lose my dad. I was "daddy's little girl." My mother was another reason I never told. If I told someone, my dad would be taken away. I would be left with mom, and that would be far worse than anything dad had or could do to me. Mom was very controlling and was emotionally, verbally, and mentally abusive. No matter what dad did to me, I always knew he loved me. I had a fierce loyalty to my father and still to this day, even though he is gone, I love him.

Even though all that and much more happened in my childhood, I look back now and can see God's loving hand gently guiding me along the steps he had established for me.

My parents were never "religious" and didn't promote a very spiritual healthy home environment. Although for some reason, they always sent me to Sunday School and Vacation Bible School...literally dropping me off at the curb and picking me up an hour later. Now I know that God was laying a foundation for my life.

One year, during our small town celebration in Minneota, Minnesota, I entered a drawing and won a children's Christian Bible from a local church. This was the beginning of my starting to see the love of God in my life. Through that experience, I was invited to attend that church and welcomed into a church family. I started attending Sunday School, Vacation Bible School, and youth group there. God placed me on the heart of the church pastor and his family. They provided a safe environment for me to experience the love of a family in a "Godly way." This family showed me love that met my emotional, psychological and spiritual longing to be loved and accepted.

I was introduced to Jesus through these experiences. When I was a sophomore in high school, the idea of accepting Jesus as my personal Lord and Savior was introduced to me. This idea resonated with my heart. The concepts of a "loving father," an "assurance of acceptance," "forgiveness for my sins," "grace," and "peace" gave me hope. I wanted more than anything for this to be "the fix" for my abusive home life. Unfortunately, I didn't understand that God's plan wasn't to deliver me from my situation, but to use my circumstances as a testimony of his love, grace, mercy, forgiveness, and power to heal.

Just like when we ignore the bolt in our tire and have to keep adding air to the tire, we can ignore the real problem...and think we only need to rely on finding a solution. I was living my life just that way. I was filling my life up with things instead of addressing the real bolt in my life. I was a Christian but was not walking with the Lord. I was using the false identity I found through my schooling at the University of Sioux Falls, my career, my achievements, and my works as the air to fill up my tire. I fell into the trap that so many people do, thinking if I did more, achieved more, and was successful (according to society's standards) I would find joy, peace and healing. As you can probably guess, I didn't have joy, peace, or healing. I struggled with anxiety, depression, hopelessness and a sinful life of promiscuity and drinking. Pouring myself completely into everything in an attempt to avoid the real issue.

Through the years I kept filling my tire with air, not truly addressing "the bolt" and planning my own course until my father died. At that point, life spiraled out of control, and I tried to commit suicide. At the time of my father's death, I was active in a different church due to attending college out of state. Shortly after being released from the hospital, I experienced a traumatic event at that church. At the time of my life where I needed to be shown the love of God more than anything, I was told by the pastor that because of my depression, anxiety and suicide attempt, "I was too sick to be in their church and did not need to return." This was devastating. If the pastor was the representation of God on earth, God's servant, God's hands and feet and that pastor says "I'm too sick," then God is saying "I'm too sick" for him too. This experience caused me to doubt and fear God, people, and the church. At that point I had no clue how much God loves "broken people" and how far from the truth it was believing "I was too sick."

Fast forward to November of 2015. I had moved to Watertown and gotten married. My career brought me to Watertown, where I hoped to have a fresh start. An opportunity to move past my history in a new location with new people. Unfortunately, I still had that bolt in my tire. Air was leaking, and the tire kept going flat. I hadn't patched my tire and dealt with the real problem. Overtime, the God shaped void in my life started to become more and more visible. He was calling me back home. How do I trust him? How do I trust the church? How do I trust a pastor again? The emptiness became too much, and I finally broke down and accepted an invite to attend church. That's when I was introduced to *Encounter*. They appeared safe from the outside, but

I had learned my lesson. I was not going to be real and authentic. I was not going to let anyone in (especially God or a pastor). I was not going to let myself be hurt again. Little did I know, God had other plans and wanted to remove the bolt from my life and patch the hole.

Once again, the Lord was establishing my steps and had something much better planned for me. After a couple weeks of dealing, or do I say not dealing with life, I reached out to *Encounter's* Pastor Paul Kimball in April of 2016. God was wanting to remove the bolt and patch the hole. I was dealing with anxiety, depression, shame, guilt, and anger, feelings of hopelessness, unworthiness, and being lost. Thankfully God gave me the desire to stop heading down the road of lies and destruction. For the first time I was exposed to the concept of my "identity in Christ." I received the truth that I was a daughter of the King of Kings and the Lord of Lords. I was priceless. I was worthy. I was clean. I was introduced to what it really meant to be in a relationship with Christ. I started walking with the Lord and developed a life of prayer, worship, time in the word, fellowship, and intimacy with my heavenly Father. God used Paul to show me there was hope, a plan, a purpose, and most of all a reason to trust God again. God used the church family to help break down the wall of protection and fear I had put around my heart. He was drawing me into communion and a life of oneness with him. My tire was patched, and the bolt was removed, and it was time to move into the plan and purpose God had for me.

Move now to January 2017. Keep in mind my tire was patched and the bolt was removed. As we all know though, patches are not permanent fixes. The only permanent fix is to allow God to heal you. Surrender to his ability to remove the old damaged tire and replace it with a new creation. 2 Corinthians 5:17 says... "Therefore, if anyone is in Christ, the new creation has come: The old has gone, the new is here!" Little did I know, changing my tire was going to be a painful experience. Thankfully from April 2016 to January 2017, God had prepared me. I had heard God's voice multiple times speak to me. He had revealed his love to me and had shown me my worth. However, I was still trying to control my steps instead of following the plan established by the Lord. I began to experience some depression and added anxiety. The lack of trust was coming back. The feelings of hopelessness and lack of trust started to take hold. My marriage was falling apart, and it seemed destined for disaster. I was starting to believe the lies of Satan that were speaking so much louder than the loving, gentle voice of God. When I did hear God, the lies were so deeply seeded that I doubted God's voice.

I remember vividly a very hard day. I was tired, not just physically but also mentally, emotionally, and spiritually. I reached out to Pastor Paul. He listened, he understood, and did his best to speak life into me. However, I wanted nothing to do with it. I felt like I had reached a breaking point. I was questioning the purpose of life and how God could use me...a broken, shattered, weak human...for anything good or purposeful. Even though I could not see it, the Lord was still establishing my steps. Paul could see this and prayed for me without ceasing during this very difficult time. When I had this realization, I was honestly and incredibly mad at Paul and God. I asked Paul to stop praying for me because it wasn't worth it. I had lost heart. Thankfully he didn't listen to me and didn't honor my wishes. God's love was relentless during this time of uncertainty. He pursued me like a shepherd calling his lost sheep home. Little did I know God was going to start revealing tiny glimpses of a path...a purpose in my life for my brokenness, my abuse, my depression, my anxiety, and so much more that had happened in my life. He was weaving together a story of hope and healing that could only be possible through His mighty power.

During this time, I also felt God calling me to return home back to where it all began, back to the church and family that started me on my path. God was going to use them to change my tire to a new one. I attended church, and it was very apparent God had destined me to go home that Sunday. The message was from the twelfth chapter of Revelations and was all about the battles of life, the battle between good and evil that started back in the Garden of Eden and continues to this day. God used the sermon to speak directly to my heart. The Holy Spirit took the knowledge, which I had heard before, and moved it for the first time the 18 inches from my head to my heart. What I was experiencing was a spiritual battle not because of me and what I had or hadn't done but because of whose I was. Satan and God were fighting over me. The great thing was that this battle was not mine, and it had been won. God was victorious and Satan knew that. That was why he was fighting so hard. My only job was to rest in the eye of the storm and keep my eyes on Jesus. Richard Alleine says, "A true Christian has his enemies under his feet even while he is in the fight. He is a soldier as soon as he is a saint, and he is a conqueror as soon as he is a soldier. His very taking up arms ensures his victory." Coming to this realization was my tire changing moment. God and his love broke through in a new and powerful way.

In life we are always going to have those bolts, nails, or screws that are going to be on the road and will get stuck in our tire. The question is, "Am I going to allow God to change the tire and create a new creation, or am I going to ignore the problem and keep filling it with air or patch it myself under my own power?" No matter how hard we plan and try to control our lives, God is the only one who can fix and heal us. We need to surrender to his working to heal us and his will. We can rest in the knowledge that God is the "Master Mechanic" and can heal and restore anything. He has only the best plans and steps established for us. We can be assured of this through his Word. Jeremiah 29:11 says, "For I know the plans I have for you," declares the Lord, "plans to prosper you and not to harm you, plans to give you hope and a future." All of these things, I desired from the very beginning.

"If the vine bent but didn't break,
then the branch was alive-abiding in the vine.
I think god bends you and me from time to time."

"And after you have suffered a little while, the God of all grace, who has called you to his eternal glory in Christ, will himself restore, confirm, strengthen, and establish you."

1 Peter 5:10

Jo's Story

During the 16 years Tony and I lived in Florida, 22 hurricanes struck the state. After Hurricane Andrew in 1992, I rode in the Miami-Dade police helicopter over Homestead and saw first-hand the devastation it caused. It was unbelievable. Buildings, house trailers, tractor trailers and yachts were tossed and thrown about like they were Tinker Toys. I've never seen anything like it. Mike Byrd, a friend of ours who lived and policed in South Florida was working when Andrew hit and he said this..."*The children of Andrew grew up overnight. The innocence they lost will never be returned.*"

Andrew was a Category 5 hurricane and it killed 65 people and left another 250,000 people homeless. It single-handedly destroyed 80% of the real estate in South Florida. A hurricane is one of the most destructive forces of nature on earth. Torrential rains and the ocean's surf, coupled with straight winds and wind gusts can completely wipeout a region. The effects are almost always catastrophic.

Tony and I will never forget our last year in Florida. It was 2004 and we lived and worked through 4 back-to-back hurricanes. We couldn't escape the mayhem. AND you wonder why we decided to stay in Watertown after retiring from police work? We'll take a blizzard over a hurricane any day of the week. The havoc—destruction—devastation—caused by a hurricane is in a very real sense the same kind of stuff children experience when they are sexually abused...When a child—through absolutely no fault of their own—is sexually abused...it pierces their very soul. It is a violation of the sanctity and wholeness of human life and when the sexual abuser is a family member or someone the child trusts— the wound is even more severe! I want you to think about this... "We are defined by relationships...we are relational to the very core of our beings. Because we are created in the image of God who is not solitary but a Trinity of Persons in love" (Father Denis Meier).

Jesus said, "If anyone causes one of these little ones—those who believe in me—to stumble, it would be better for them to have a large millstone hung around their neck and to be drowned in the depth of the sea" (Matthew 18:6). Jesus said that because He knows how precious and vulnerable children are...He knows the importance of good and loving relationships and family ties. Jesus knows...

Did you know only 11% of Child Sexual Abuse (CSA) incidents are committed by a stranger? The majority of CSA incidents happen in relationship with a family member or someone else known by the child or family. In years gone by, law enforcement taught—*Stranger Danger*—but we had it wrong—because the majority of time the sex offender is NOT a stranger but someone who lives right up under our noses!

The first evidence-based research on Adverse Childhood Experiences happened in 1998. Since then, there have been 57 other publications through 2011. We have 13 years of current evidence-based research available to help us. So, we know the effects of Adverse Childhood Experiences. You can go online and Google—"Take the ACE Quiz" to get your own score. A-C-E, ACE is the acronym for Adverse Childhood Experiences. There is staggering proof that health, social and economic risks are the result of childhood trauma! For instance...we know...

> If you have an ACE score of 1 or more, you have an increased risk of cancer, heart disease, depression and obesity.
> If you have an ACE score of 6 and higher, your life span is almost 2 decades shorter than those with a score of zero.
> If you have an ACE score of 7 or 8, you're 3 times more likely to have cardiovascular disease as an adult.

We know that toxic stress damages the developing brain architecture and can lead to life-long problems in learning, behavior, and physical and mental health. AND that early high stress experiences imbed into the body with lifelong cognitive, emotional and physical health effects. Because of the research that has been done, we know there are correlations between CSA and social issues such as abortion, alcohol and drug addictions, divorce, eating disorders, human-trafficking, promiscuity, prostitution, self-harm, self-injury, self-mutilation and suicide...

I'm convinced that child abuse and especially—CSA is an underlying cause of many social issues we face today. That's worth repeating—CSA is the root cause of social issues. I think it's the reason so many people suffer from depression and addictions.

Let me share with you some statistics in the State of South Dakota: At least 4,000 children experience sexual abuse in South Dakota each year. 1 in 4 females and 1 in 6 males are sexually abused every year before the age of 18. The overwhelming majority of victims are Caucasian.

It's an epidemic that has got to stop! AND we're the ones who can make a difference! As Christians, we understand it is the presence and love of the Trinity that helps transform us individually and as community. AND this kind of transformation can take place only in a community of love—such as ours.

Did you know that in the City of Watertown every three days, someone threatens suicide, attempts suicide, or commits suicide? Now clearly, committing suicide is the lower of the three, but even so, that seems awfully high to me...always has!

In October 2007, I lost my best friend, Trina Whiting to suicide—she pulled her car into her garage, closed the door and left it running. When Tony and I got the "late night phone call", I cried myself to sleep that night. As a young girl, Trina was raped several times and each time it happened—he wounded her soul. The experts say that everyone reacts differently...some "fight," some run—they call that "flight"...and others "freeze." Trina ran as fast as she could to escape the memories but they continued to haunt her and she just gave up. I'll always love Trina.

I am so grateful for Governor Dennis Daugaard who in 2014 appointed Jolene's Law Task Force to confront and tackle CSA head-on. Watertown has been chosen as the location—to headquarter a Multi-Disciplinary Team to investigate and combat CSA in Northeast South Dakota. Lake Area Tech is being used to help train the officers and investigators on CSA investigation protocol. That's exciting! And Watertown's Sanford Clinic is serving as the location for a child's advocacy center—no longer will families and law enforcement have to travel to Sioux Falls for a forensic interview. Together...with God's help...we can and will make a difference.

As a community, we can't afford to not talk about CSA. We can't afford to play that old game of...see no evil, hear no evil, speak no evil. There's too much at stake because the lives of our kids are hanging in the balance. This CSA stuff is generational. It gets passed on from one generation to the next...and for too long those who have been brave enough to disclose have been silenced by their own family members. I've heard too many tell me, "My mom or dad, my grandparents or brothers and sisters told me, 'To just get over it and let it go.'" Bringing it up just upsets the applecart and Lord knows...we wouldn't want to do that... Our silence is killing people. We have to start believing our kids when they disclose to us.

When I first came to Watertown, I met Dick Stricherz. Like many of you, I love Dick...he was a "one of kind." Before he passed away this past November, Dick gave me three of his books and some of the training materials he had on alcoholism and sexual abuse. Dick loved to share his personal story with my Criminal Justice Students at Mount Marty College and Lake Area Tech. Dick was a school teacher too and he taught Substance Abuse classes at both schools. Dick was sexually abused as a little boy and those horrendous acts against his soul wounded him immensely. Dick was an alcoholic and he was so proud of his 40 years of sobriety. Dick also suffered bouts of depression and contemplated suicide on more than one occasion.

Each time I heard Dick tell his story to my students, the Holy Spirit worked in and through Dick to transform me. That's the power of community, the power of love. Because it is the presence and love of the Trinity that transforms us individually and as a community. Dag Hammarskjold once wrote: "The longest journey of any person is the journey inward, and that longest journey is the eighteen inches from the head to the heart."

Each time Dick told his story, I processed his words in my head BUT it was the Holy Spirit who caused my heart to burn. God transformed Dick's brokenness into a flame-tempered vessel to carry His fire...a fire which ignited my heart. I've asked the Holy Spirit to use me as a flame-tempered vessel. I've asked the Holy Spirit to ignite your hearts with the fire of God causing it to burn in your memories and your hearts forever. It's been said, "Never be afraid when God brings back your past. Let your memory have its way with you. It is a minister of God bringing its rebuke and sorrow to you. God will turn what might have been into a wonderful lesson of growth for the future" (Oswald Chambers).

Like Dick, I too was sexually abused as a little girl and although I've experienced many dark nights of the soul through it all God saved me. I don't know how young I was when the abuse started—perhaps I was four or five years old, maybe younger. It didn't happen all the time just some of the time—whenever we went to my grandmother's house for the weekend. My Dad was gone for most of my early life or at least that's the way it seemed to me. The first time I remember seeing Dad, I was five or six years old. On the day he came home from overseas, I remember seeing a large group of soldiers exiting a very large, green, military airplane. All the men looked similar as they were wearing army fatigues. As they walked closer, across the tarmac, I wondered which one of the men would be my father? Even though Dad came home from Korea, the abuse continued whenever we'd go for a weekend visit to grandmother's house. My abuser was my uncle, my dad's oldest brother. Uncle Elmo never married and lived with my grandparents. Everybody said he was an alcoholic.

The sexual abuse is too distasteful for me to talk about it publicly. Just know that my uncle sexually, mentally and emotionally abused me. You may be wondering—Where was Jesus when all of this was going on? I will tell you that He was right there with me—and every time he slayed me—he slayed Jesus too. Jesus didn't get me out of it BUT He got me through it. Unexpectedly, Uncle Elmo dies shortly after I turn nine years old. Prior to his death, I never told anyone about the abuse, other than my best friend, Lisa who was only one year older than me. Neither one of us knew exactly what to do! So, we just keep the secret between ourselves—best friends forever—even to this very day.

Almost a year passed by since Uncle Elmo's death. I was 10 and my mother ordered a series of booklets purposed to help me understand the facts of life, you know, the "birds and the bees." So, I read the booklets and, for the first time, I grasp what Uncle Elmo did to me. Naively, I assume I'm pregnant. Again, I tell Lisa, my best friend. Still, we don't know what to do! So, I go to bed that night petrified and scared to death. I cry with my head buried in my pillow so as not to make any noise.

On that evening, my mom came into my bedroom as she always did to offer a good night's kiss at which time mom discovered me crying. Mom asks, "What's the matter? Why are you crying?" I blurt out, "I'm pregnant!" AND then, I sat on the foot my bed and told my mom in detail how Uncle Elmo, who had been dead for almost a year, had sexually abused me.

I think that was the longest night of my life. When the interview stopped, the drama began. Then, everybody knew what had happened to me—my mother, father, siblings, grandparents, aunts, uncles, cousins, and neighbors—ALL knew what Uncle Elmo did to me. Everyone was angry BUT there was no one to punish because he was already dead. There was a lot of chaos— uproar, disbelief and a lot of shame going around. Mom and Dad openly argued and debated the matter. Ultimately, Dad said, "He couldn't believe that his brother would do such a thing."

My father's words were clear. They cut me deeply creating

a gaping wound, which bled for many years. In my parents' ignorance, there was no doctor's visit, no police report, no investigation, no counseling, NO NOTHING! There was just a little girl...me...who felt abandoned, shame, humiliation, isolation and disgrace! Do you get the picture? It was a real quagmire! There was nothing, absolutely nothing, except for God's grace! In the book of Isaiah, the prophet tells us, "Cry for help and you'll find its grace and more grace. The moment he hears, he'll answer." (Isaiah 30:19)

When there was nothing, absolutely nothing, but God's grace, God's grace shaped and saved me. God gave me treasures of darkness and riches hidden in secret places. (Isaiah 45:3) He called me by name and it was His strength and it, alone which gave me everything I needed to rise above my circumstance. God gave me people, places and experiences like you wouldn't believe. God's grace gave me courage, wisdom and strength. He gave me teachers and preachers who served as major role models in my life.

I grew up in the Southern Baptist Church. Looking back, I exhibited behaviors indicative of CSA that should have been obvious, but it was the 1960s and they didn't know then what we know now. God knew the direction I was headed. I was about 12 years old, when God used my girlfriend, Lisa, again. She invited me to Methodist Youth Fellowship. Since my mom grew up in the Methodist Church, she allowed me to go and ultimately, I was baptized and joined the Asbury United Methodist Church when I was 13 years old. We had an awesome youth group and the pastor was a second father to us-wayward kids. At the age of 15, I felt that God was calling me into the ministry. So, I began discerning God's call. I skipped my last year of high school and entered college at 16 years of age. I was just 18, in college working on a License to Preach with the Methodist Church, when I ran into a roadblock, a detour.

An old district superintendent—thought that I should think about another career path other than the ministry because I was a female. At that time, women had not yet broken the barrier in the Methodist Church—the glass ceiling was still in-tack in South Georgia.

Then, my oldest brother—a staunch Southern Baptist called me "out of the blue" and told me that he wanted to take me to lunch. At the time, I was away to LaGrange College where I was studying Religion. It was mid-January 1977. I thought my brother wanted to take me out for a congratulatory lunch due to a recent Christmas engagement and the award of a scholarship to go to Jerusalem for the upcoming summer. Like the ole district superintendent, Jack told me that women aren't supposed to be preachers and furthermore...the fella I was engaged to was a looser! Somewhere, in the middle of our lunch date, I zoned my brother out. I thought to myself: "Now, you want to tell me how to live my life. Where were you when I needed you?"

I remember sitting on a grassy hillside that evening and starring across the landscape of the college campus for what seemed like hours. I was perplexed and distraught. There was an anger inside of me that was raging like a storm. At the time, I was working on the weekends as a youth pastor at the Rose Hill United Methodist Church. My boss, Reverend Max Barlow was the man who baptized me. Max was like a father to me. I wanted to talk with him about the district superintendent and my brother but we never got the chance because Max was going through his own crisis. Max had an affair with the church secretary. He was married and so was she at the time and it was a huge scandal in the church. Max left the ministry. I told Max that I didn't care about all the gossip—that I'd always love him. He just looked at me with tears in his eyes and never said a word otherwise.

Those collective experiences rocked my core. Ultimately, I withdrew from college and I quit being a youth director. I threw in the towel. I remember walking out of the church office. I was just standing there in the church parking lot in a confused state of mind. I looked up and I yelled at God, "What in the world am I supposed to do?" Immediately, a black and white police car drove past and a female was driving the car. She rolled up to the stop sign; the window was down. She had blonde hair and it was up in a French braid. She came to a stop, had her blinker on, and she made a right turn and she drove out of sight. It was no more than a five second encounter. I thought, "that's what I'll do...I'll be a police officer." So, that week, I made application and a few months later they hired me.

I should have gotten on my knees BUT, instead I copped an attitude. I had a chip on my shoulder. I thumbed my nose up at God and church. Pride and anger got in my way; I focused on my circumstances and NOT on God. I decided that I knew what was best for my life. I was hurt and mad and became defiant...the storm within me erupted. I went into police work and I never looked back. I fell from God's grace like I had jumped off the Empire State Building.

For about 10 years of my life, throughout my twenties, I lost my way. I stopped walking in the presence of Jesus. I saw and experienced things that caused my heart to grow cold and calloused. I became indifferent to God. Police work exposed me to a very dark side of humanity. My faith weakened slowly. I didn't pray. I didn't read my Bible. I didn't go to church.

I'd like to go back for just a minute to repeat what I was telling you about the importance of relationships. We are created in God's image—3 Persons in Love! We are relational to the core. But when you are sexually abused as a little kid—it messes you up —the sticky-adhesive stuff on your *Band-Aid* doesn't work like it's supposed to. You don't trust easily—your guard is up—you're super vigilant all the time. Frankly, my thought process during that time of my life was this—"It will be a cold day in hell before I let another son-of-a-gun hurt me again." Nowadays, the professionals would say that I suffered from PTSD—post-traumatic stress disorder or "wounded attachments." You see, the very act of CSA damages a child's ability to trust...to have healthy relationships with people, with community and with God. Child sexual abuse not only damages one's physical body and mental/ cognitive mind-set, but also disrupts one's spiritual being. That's not the way God intended it to be.

But God does all things well. When I look back on my life, I realize that police work was a good fit for me. I had the ability to set my emotions aside and not let anything touch me. The numbness came naturally for me. I was a good cop. I did my job well, but in those early days of my career, I was lost, I was alone, I was afraid and no one, but God knew how dark my soul.

During this dark time of my life, I got pregnant out of wedlock and had an abortion. I was in and out of several relationships and police work was the only thing that made sense in my life. My personal life was a wreck but I thought that, as long as, I have my job, I can make it. I can survive. One night I was working and didn't have any business working that night...but there I was. I was going through a divorce. I caught my ex-cheating on me and it just ripped me apart. My Lieutenant, whom I respected, told me that I should get over it. He said, "You need to get over it"—I had heard that line before. I should "just get over" everything and pretend that nothing ever happened. I remember sitting in my squad car on a gravel road. It was early morning about 3 AM and I started thinking about everything—it all came back and piled up like a ton of bricks on my shoulders: the sexual abuse, my father not believing me, my mother not protecting me, my family emotionally abandoning me, the church turning me away, failed relationships, abortion, divorce...and I concluded that I was a failure. So, I pulled my 357 Smith and Wesson Magnum out of my holster and stuck it in my mouth and I tried to pull the trigger but God wouldn't let me. I yelled at God and told Him to "just leave me the hell alone."

Then, I got a radio call from headquarters. I holstered my gun and picked up the mic. I swallowed hard and cleared my voice so that no one could "hear" that I had been crying: "Headquarters, this is 113 go ahead with the call." They dispatched me to a verbal domestic at a trailer park. I acknowledged the call, wiped my face and responded to the call. When I got there, this couple—a guy and a girl were arguing because the guy caught her "running around" on him. He was crying and carrying on. I ended up cuffing him and putting him in the backseat of my squad car.

On the way to the jail, I kept looking in my rearview mirror at his face. I could feel his pain. I started crying with him because I knew exactly how he felt. I pulled over and stopped my car. I opened the back door and told him to get out of my car. I told him to turn around and I took the cuffs off him. I stood on the side of the road crying with and hugging this man whom I had arrested. I told him that I was sorry that his girlfriend cheated on him. I let him go and asked him to not go back to the house that night. He promised me that he wouldn't go back there AND then, I drove away and back to the gravel road.

Again, I pulled my gun out and put it in my mouth. I knew that letting the man go was totally improper but I didn't care...I didn't care about anything. BUT God wouldn't let me pull the trigger...

On that particular night Jesus ran to me...He sought me and saved me because I was lost! On that road that night, there was a calm in the mix of my emotional turmoil and I could hear the **still small voice** of Jesus telling me—"I know everything and I love you."

In my brokenness, I realized Jesus loved me despite all my sins and all my failings—despite everything that I did and failed to do, Jesus loved me—unconditionally—no matter what.

God doesn't love us because we're good, or even because we're worthy. God loves us—because Christ is in us and nothing can separate us from Christ.

So, I began my journey back home from the far country with the dirt of the pigpen still on my soul. It was Archbishop Fulton Sheen who said, "There are two ways of knowing how good God is: one is never to lose Him, and the other is to lose Him and then to find Him."

I moved to Florida in 1989 and Tony and I met in 1990. I fell in love with a Baltimore Cradle Catholic! Three years later we married in December 1993. For the first time in my life, God helped me to give my heart completely to another person—unconditionally. I trusted him. He helped me to work through some of the issues I had from being sexually abused as a child. We made it a priority to pray and to go to church. That's how I became a Catho-Metho-Bapterian. I've been ecumenical all of my life.

Some very awesome priests helped to shepherd me into a personal relationship with Jesus Christ for 16 years in Florida. AND for the past 12 years here in South Dakota, Father Denny Meier and the Sisters of the Mother of God Monastery have been my spiritual guides.

This journey that we're on is a lifetime process of repentance, surrender and obedience. Since finding God again—He has reconciled my relationships with my father and mother before they passed away in 2010 and 2013. Two days before I turned 55, I got a phone call that my mother was dying—she had suffered with Alzheimer's for 10 years. I flew to Atlanta on Friday. Rented a car and drove directly to the hospice center. All the way, I prayed over and over—Lord, please let me get to my mother's bedside before she dies. I need to be there! God gave me 3 days with my mother. I turned 55 on Sunday, and Mom died on Monday. For 3 days, in my mother's room...we experienced God's grace. Mom and I talked and walked together as she journeyed to the other side. As I held my mother's hand, I knew that I was holding Christ's hand and that my hand, was for her—Christ's hand. We were in effect Jesus for each other. The Incarnate Word became flesh in us. As she drew her last breath, her eyes opened and rolled in a circular motion and became fixed looking up. I know she saw God's bright light. Grace rushed over me like never before and I was at total peace in Christ.

The next day, it was a Tuesday, I took a drive with my middle brother and his wife to Thomaston, Georgia—the place where I had been abused. I asked my brother to drive to my Grandmother's house, the house where I had been abused so many times by my uncle. It had been 46 years since I went to that place. The house was no longer there. It was gone. It was completely gone! I had nothing to fear. I can't tell you how many times I've walked through that house in my mind.

On Thursday, we buried mom and on Friday, I flew back to Watertown. On Saturday, the Watertown Police Department's annual awards banquet occurred. Because it was my last year as Chief of Police, I was the keynote speaker. I delivered a heartfelt talk and gave my officers some lasting words of wisdom. All three of our chaplains were there. After I delivered my message, Father Denny jumped up and hugged me. Then, the Lutheran pastor,

Janine Rew-Werling asked me, right then and there, if I would fill in for her on April 7. She said, "I have somewhere I need to be. Will you preach for me on April 7?" I couldn't believe my ears. God worked through that Lutheran pastor and invited me back into the pulpit. As soon as she asked me, I said, "Are you serious?" Then, I said, "Yes." Talk about a Holy Curveball. I retired on April 1st and on April 7th, I stood in the pulpit for the first time in 37 years. God is amazing. The experience knocked my stocks off. I can't adequately explain the immense love that I felt and it didn't matter to me one iota that I was a woman, a Catholic preaching in a Lutheran Church. What mattered was that God saved me, God restored me, God could use me—the worst of sinners—to be a vessel for His fire. How thankful I am to Christ Jesus, our Lord for choosing me as one of His messengers, and giving me the strength to be faithful to Him. (1 Timothy 1:12-13).

God has given me the grace to forgive my uncle. He has given me the assurance that my named child, Jacob Joseph, whom I aborted is with Him and that I'll get to meet him one day.

If you're suffering, I urge you to lay your pain and suffering at the foot of the cross. God's time is not the same as our time. But we can rest assured that our God does all things well. In 1 Peter, chapter 5, verse 10, we are told: "And after you have suffered a little while, the God of all grace, who has called you to his eternal glory in Christ, will himself restore, confirm, strengthen, and establish you."

Then, you and I must choose whether we are here to save our lives or to give our lives in service to the world for Christ's sake. We must make up our minds whether we're going to go through life holding hands with ourselves or reach out to help the hurt of the world. Have you ever noticed what Jesus does when you give him a loaf of bread? He reaches out—he takes the bread—says the blessing—breaks the bread and gives it. And so it is with my life, Jesus took me—He blessed me—He broke me—and He shares me—uses me—works in, with, and through me to help others know him.

God led Tony and I to create a fund at the *Watertown Area Community Foundation* to benefit children who have been sexually abused—whenever a child discloses sexual abuse to law enforcement—they give the child/caregiver a card that refers them to *Joy Ranch* for an equine experience to begin the healing process. *Chief Jo's Hope, Healing and Hoof Prints* serves 13 counties and Sisseton Wahpeton Tribe in Northeast South Dakota. In June of 2016, *Hope In God* came into being. It's a Christian network of women survivors of child sexual abuse and sexual assault who provide spiritual and emotional support to each other while increasing community awareness in Northeast South Dakota. We're anchored at *Joy Ranch*.

Our Lord never works just through one individual. He always works through a community of individuals to accomplish His purpose. *Hope In God* serves as a resource for law enforcement and churches and provides six offerings to survivors of child sexual abuse and sexual assault: weekly <u>Wounded Heart</u> book study here at Cornerstone; one-on-one mentoring offering; outreach awareness opportunities for churches, businesses, schools and organizations; indoor and outdoor activities; weekly circle groups; and, diversity initiatives. Most recently, we have initiated *Hope In God* for men.

I began by talking about hurricanes and the destruction that they cause. One of the peculiar features of a hurricane is the eye which can be found in the midst of every hurricane. There is calm in the eye of every storm and so it is in the realm of the Holy Spirit. In the center of the tempests of life we can find a place of quiet communion in the Holy Spirit. That is the place where God dwells and in Him there is perfect peace. But how do we get there? How do we stay hopeful after being wounded? How do we pass through the turmoil—the hurt—the anger—the shame—the brokenness—the humiliation of child sexual abuse? Jesus sought and saved me on a gravel road.

God always rescues His people when they recognize their own brokenness—it is then that God unleashes His full power. When we try to solve problems independently of God, His work is impeded. Every trial that enters our life comes thru His permissive will—He is in control and He will see us through it. BUT we must...

1. We keep our eyes fixed on Jesus—We must ponder the Person of Jesus Christ—in doing so we begin to know Him as He reveals Himself to us. It is only in knowing Jesus that we can begin to become like Jesus, and becoming Christ-like is the purpose of our daily walk of faith.

2. Apart from Jesus, we can do nothing—As long as we abide in Him, He produces His fruit in us. The fruit is not for the good of the branch but for those who come to carry it away. A fruit bearing tree lives not for itself but wholly for those to whom its fruit brings refreshment and life.

My grandmother used to grow Scuppernongs & Muscadines on her farm in Georgia. They're a type of grape that grows well in the south and boy are they good! As kids, we loved to pick them and eat them right off the vine. Each fall, grandmother would prune the vines to ensure a good crop for the next year. To do so, she'd have to determine which branch was alive or not. It's almost impossible just by looking at a branch to determine if it's dead or alive. The only way grandmother could tell was by bending branch. If it broke off, then there is no sap going into it. If it bent but didn't break, then the branch was alive —abiding in the vine. I think God bends you and me from time to time, to see if we are attached to the vine. Only those who are attached will produce fruit because they're being fed by the vine.

I'm convinced God gave me 36 years in law enforcement—as "time in the desert" where He bent and pruned me. He opened my eyes and ears and gave me experiences to transform my heart fashioning me to be able to fulfill His purpose. When Saint John of the Cross wanted to call to mind the greatest heights of union with God, he compared it to a wood log being burned away by fire. When we practice the presence of God, He transforms us like a glowing log that is so united with the fire that it is the fire.

Tony and I have a backyard fire pit that we really enjoy. I've noticed that as we add a piece of wood to the fire and it begins to burn, it becomes one with the fire, being transformed into light and heat and energy. In the process, it is consumed and changed into something it was not there before: carbon ash. It will never be a piece of wood again. That's how God transforms us and prepares to send us out. With the fire of love smoldering in our hearts—we are ready for the outward journey—which will take us into our community living lives of sacrifice and service. AND any good that we do is because He first touched us—He changed us—He transformed you and me. I will always carry the scar of CSA but it is no longer a weeping wound. Christ has removed the poison and all that is left is the mark. God has given me the grace to show you my wounds.

Our Lord never hid his wounds or concealed them, instead Jesus showed them and allowed the Apostle Thomas to touch his wounds. Jesus gives us the courage to show and allow others to touch our wounds. Whatever your circumstances are...sexual assault or abuse, alcohol/drug addictions, cancer/other illness... death of loved one...loss of a job...maybe you have had an abortion, maybe you've abused someone, perhaps your worried about a friend/loved one...I want you to know that God loves you and that His mercy and grace are greater than any of your circumstances or sins. Our Lord, "Jesus wants you to bring your festering wound into His Light so that He can heal them to be touched by others" (Sheila Walsh). We need not fear because everywhere our Savior leads us He precedes us. AND we have the assurance that nothing can separate us from the love of God in Jesus Christ.

I'll close with the words of Apostle Paul: "Do you think anyone is going to be able to drive a wedge between us and Christ's love for us? There is no way! Not trouble, not hard times, not hatred, not hunger, not homelessness, not bullying threats, not backstabbing, not even the worst sins listed in Scripture...I'm absolutely convinced that nothing—nothing living or dead, angelic or demonic, today or tomorrow, high or low, thinkable or unthinkable—absolutely nothing can get in between us and God's love because of the way that Jesus our Master has embraced us." (Romans 8:35, 37-39). (Eugene Peterson-The Message)

May the love and peace of Christ be with you, always.

ABOUT THE ILLUSTRATIONS

In February 2017, after our first Hope in God Winter Retreat was completed, it became clear that a compilation of women's stories of surviving the trauma of childhood sexual abuse and assault would spring forth. At the time, Jo Vitek asked me to create the cover for this book. When I am asked to do a project of any kind, my mind immediately takes off – like spontaneous combustion – an internal brainstorm commences with a direction and propulsion all its own. I hold this process lightly letting the Spirit guide my thoughts and prayers around the project, knowing full well a co-creative process with God ensures the most desirable result.

In the beginning of May 2017, I came up with a "rough draft" of the cover for this book to share with others involved in the *Courageous Women* project. As the stories were written, Jo and I both concluded that an illustration for each story would help the stories come alive. Wow! What was I thinking? Fourteen illustrations to complete with a short deadline is no small feat! I put the production of the cover on the back burner and turned to each woman's story. My task was to illustrate that moment or moments when God spoke the truth of their dignity, their beauty, and broke through their woundedness to reveal the one True Hope for healing – healing of their mind, heart, soul and strength. I thought maybe the collection of illustrations would change what had been swirling in my mind for the cover...but it did not. It only enhanced and affirmed the image I had received months earlier.

What I found in each woman's story was the voice of Truth, the voice of the Spirit of God speaking loud and clear in their lives, and into our lives. In Isaiah 11:1-2 we hear that *courage* is a gift of the Holy Spirit. It is *courage* that helps us to overcome fear and step forward as a follower of Jesus Christ - to do what is right in the sight of God and others. A *woman of courage* has the conviction of heart and mind that is required for both doing good and enduring evil. Each of these women possesses courage they never knew they had, but God did; God put it within them.

I wanted the cover to summarize the stories, as a collective. For this reason, I chose to incorporate the following: The *woman of courage* is facing into the South Dakota wind, a symbol of the *ruah* or breath of God present not just from the beginning of all time (Gen. 1:1) but in the "now" of each second of our lives. The bird is the Spirit of Truth being spoken aloud by the woman for, Truth can only be seen and heard in the "light of day" so we might perceive that God is doing something new as the results spring forth! (Isaiah 43:19) In fact, the "light of day" is a prairie sunrise, a new day, almost always so brilliant and exquisitely colored one must conclude that only God can be the artist. Her face is relaxed, her eyes are closed because she is at peace, a deep peace a result of abiding in the Truth of the Spirit of God (Gal 5:22-23). In her hair is a dream catcher, the neotraditional symbol of Native American culture, most of us are familiar with. Clearly the cross of Christ is in the center of this dream catcher. For our Native American sisters and brothers, a dream catcher is thought to protect innocents from spirits that could harm them. Most survivors express feelings of great vulnerability and exposure to being harmed at any time; but now Jesus Christ has become the focus of their lives and His steadfast love is what upholds and protects them.

To read and pray with the story of each woman, listening for the voice of the Spirit of God has been an honor and a blessing! It is my hope and prayer that in some small way the illustrations of this book help you to see and hear the Spirit of Truth all around you, in all circumstances and in every situation of your life. May you too be lifted by the courage God put within you, able to overcome fear, stepping forward as a follower of Jesus Christ.

Sr. Barbara Younger, OSB
www.benedictinearts.org

Contact:
Jo Vitek
HopeinGodwatertownsd@gmail.com
FB @watertownHIGtrees
www.HopeinGodweb.wordpress.com
605-880-6201
525 South Lake Drive, Watertown, SD 57201

67130198R00078

Made in the USA
Lexington, KY
02 September 2017